UNLIMITED SPORTS SUCCESS

Unlimited Sports Success

The Power of Hypnosis

Stephen Mycoe

Writers Club Press
San Jose New York Lincoln Shanghai

Unlimited Sports Success
The Power of Hypnosis

All Rights Reserved © 2001 by Stephen Mycoe

No part of this book may be reproduced or transmitted in any form or by any means, graphic, electronic, or mechanical, including photocopying, recording, taping, or by any information storage retrieval system, without the permission in writing from the publisher.

Writers Club Press
an imprint of iUniverse.com, Inc.

For information address:
iUniverse.com, Inc.
5220 S 16th, Ste. 200
Lincoln, NE 68512
www.iuniverse.com

Although inspired by actual events, the names, persons, and characters in this publication have been altered for the protection and confidentiality of the people involved.
Any resemblance to real life people or events is purely coincidental.

ISBN: 0-595-18610-6

Printed in the United States of America

This book is dedicated to my Grandfather 'David W. Oddy'.

Contents

Acknowledgements xi
Introduction—Unlimited Sports Success. xiii
    The Power of Hypnosis xv

Part One 1
CHAPTER ONE
A BRIEF HISTORY OF HYPNOSIS—SELECTED CHRONICLES. 3
    The historic contours of hypnosis—a short navigation. 3
CHAPTER TWO
THE MIND AND BODY CONNECTION—AUTOGENIC GYMNASTICS. 9
    Mind Power—the champions mental tool box. 9
    The Placebo Effect—mind body power in action. 14
    Belief Systems—the foundations of excellence. 16
    The Will—gaining inner strength to push your body to its limits. 20
    Goal setting—the elite athletes mental microscope. 21
    Alan, 100 metre Sprinter—case study 1. 22
CHAPTER THREE
INTERNAL DIALOGUE—THE LINGUISTIC NUTRITION OF CHAMPIONS. 25
    Positive thoughts—athletic blueprint to success. 25

Self-Sabotage—reducing the fear of suffering what you fear! 28
Fear Management—sympathetic power reactors. 34
Arousal Levels—change your state, unleash performance results. 36
Ten Steps to Adjusting Arousal Levels in Sport. 38
Geoff, Bodybuilding mental blocks—case study 2. 40

CHAPTER FOUR
WHICH CHEESE IS THE MOON MADE OF?—EXPLODING THE SPORTS SPONGE. 44

Cosmetic Weight Control—energy in, energy out. 44
Motivation—life's driving force. 47
Losing Weight—weightlessly. 53
Dieting—the balancing act. 54
Hunger Signals—mind / emotion strategies. 57
Bulking up—infinite dimensions. 58
Alison, Weight Loss
—case study 3. Half a stone per week no diet changes. 59
Summary; 62
Ways to create an energy deficit; 62

Part Two 65

CHAPTER FIVE
HYPNOSIS—HUMANKIND'S DREAMWEAVER. 67

Structures of Magic—the countless perceptions of hypnosis. 67
Analytical Hypnotherapy—the precept of cause and effect. 73
Dangers of Hypnosis—taking control of your life. 74
The Syntax of Hypnosis
—how to hypnotise using hetero and auto-hypnosis. 76
Signs of Hypnosis—mother natures Bio-feedback guide. 81
Bridget, equestrian phobia/injury—Case study 4. 82

CHAPTER SIX
HYPNOTIC INDUCTIONS—MAKING THE CONNECTION. 85

Effectual Inductions—the Parasympathetic systems natural escalator. 85
Index of Inductions 87

Chapter Seven
Constructing Scripts for Sport and Life
—affirmation manifestation. 100
    Hypnotic Scripts—lyrics of transformation. *100*
    Kate, Basketball player—Case study 5. ....*104*
    Hypnotic Scripts Index. *106*
Athletic Smoking Cessation 107
Boxing Power 116
Breast Enhancement 122
Endless Endurance 127
Exceptional Golf 131
Martial Arts Spiritual Development 135
Rugby Football 140
Silky Soccer Skills 148
Sports Fear Control 157
Sports Success Programming 162
Style Improvement 166
Supreme Weight Loss 169
Top Level Tennis 183
Weight Gain for Bodybuilding 187

Notes 195
Glossary of Terms 197
Bibliography 201
About the Author 203

Acknowledgements

Thanks to Carolynne for her multiple editorial enhancements. In the unlikely event of any errors please address your complaints to her, she'd be glad for the feedback! Thanks also to all the experts who have given their technical advice on the development of scripts for individual sports, especially Ross 'Silky' Nichol's.

Introduction
—*Unlimited Sports Success.*

'Even when I went to the playground, I never picked the best players. I picked guys with less talent, but who were willing to work hard, who had the desire to be great.
—Earvin 'Magic' Johnson, NBA guard.

There is one thing that makes a champion a *Champion*, the Power of his/her mind. *That's it!* There is nothing else! Genetics, constant practice, natural ability, strength and endurance are all slaves to the mind. There is nothing in sport or any other endeavour that does not begin and end with the power of the mind. Everybody has the natural ability inside him or her NOW, to achieve absolutely anything. The traits you need mentally, emotionally and physically for success you already possess within. With the assistance of hypnosis you can gain access to these abilities and experience the reality of your potential success. You are capable of being the sports person you wish to be.

This book will introduce you to many of the mental techniques I have learned whilst working with a variety of athletes from a broad spectrum of sporting arenas. You will learn simple methods written in an accessible, practical style which will enable anyone to incorporate them into their game. Whether your desires are based in the sporting arena or any other area of your life, follow the instructions and you will achieve your potential. I have total and unreserved confidence in your abilities.

Some of the techniques that you will discover are very simple, yet used correctly extremely powerful. These are techniques used by every single successful person who has achieved anything in their life, strangely enough every single person who has ever failed to achieve his or her desires also uses the same system! We all use these techniques, although the majority of humans use them unknowingly. Therefore, a person's outcome is not always to their satisfaction.

You don't need to believe in hypnosis for it to be effective. Hypnosis is based in the Subconscious mind, the non-critical part of the psyche. There is little need for conscious acceptance, other than the desire to be helped in this manner. You will learn in this book how to gain access to past experiences of success and to duplicate those actions, whenever you wish, as often as you wish. In addition I will give you examples of the successful athletes who have used these techniques to achieve amazing results, and how they did it in case studies and custom made hypnotic scripts. You will learn how to increase your motivation, at will. How to improve style and increase your stamina. Fear and anxiety will begin to diminish. You will learn to notice and banish success sabotage and other obstacles to your performance. These may seem like extravagant claims, but believe me, follow your dreams and my instructions and together we will accomplish your ultimate sporting desires. Read this book from cover to cover, as it was designed to be read, and you will have the tools to take your sporting and everyday abilities to the next level and beyond. It is true that this book was written with the sports person in mind however, many of the techniques within are perfectly adjustable to all areas of your life. If you have bought this book and find you do not read it fully and subsequently do not act upon the ideas and techniques, you are doing yourself an injustice.

The Power of Hypnosis

- Surveys conducted on the effects of mind over matter documented that in a sample of over 800 women, 80% saw gains of over one and a half inches in breast size due to breast enhancement hypnosis.
- 1808—1859, DR James Esdaile carried out thousands of major surgery operations using Hypno-anaesthesia.
- Nazi's used hypnosis to dull pain during both world wars when their supply of Chloroform ran out.
- Major surgery; brain operations, abdominal surgery, amputations and vasectomies have all been conducted using hypno-anaesthesia, no other pain relief was required.
- Hypnosis has been found to be the most effective form of smoking cessation over any other method world-wide.
- Hypnosis releases Endorphins from the Pituitary gland in the brain—the 'happy' hormone causing a happy smiling hypnotic after the session is complete.
- Physiological changes such as reduced blood pressure and heart rate are immediate once hypnosis is attained, due to Autonomic Nervous System adjustments.
- Right brain functioning is the side predominantly used during hypnosis and is the key to accessing our behaviour motivations and past experiences.
- Hypnosis has the ability to increase visualisation skills and enhance abilities to hallucinate vividly.
- Injuries treated by hypnosis are known to heal quicker and bleeding is reduced far more effectively than by other methods.
- All forms of deep relaxation such as hypnosis increase secretion of the pineal hormone Melatonin. This is the natural drug responsible

for inhibiting the growth of many types of cancer, preventing 'free-radicals' and rejuvenating the skin as an anti-ageing treatment.
- Yogis are able to stop blood flow and their hearts beating through self-hypnosis.
- Much evidence is available of the benefits of practising Yoga (a form of hypnosis) in treating Clinical Depression and Panic attacks in humans.
- The American Psychological Association Meeting 1999 reported that children treated with hypnosis for 'Attention Deficit Disorder' gained results as effective as those from the drug Ritalin. *(Psychology Today, January 2001)*
- Pain alleviation hypnosis was successful in the treatment of 169 patients who suffered chronic tension headaches. *(International Journal of Clinical Experimental Hypnosis, 2000)*
- Athletic performance can be increased dramatically in many areas, style correction, speed and strength enhancements are particularly effective.

Part One

Chapter One

A Brief History of Hypnosis
—*selected chronicles.*

'Greatness is not in where we stand, but in which direction we are moving. We must sail sometimes with the wind and sometimes against it—but sail we must and not drift, nor lie at anchor'
—Oliver Wendell Holmes.

The historic contours of hypnosis—*a short navigation.*

Hippocrates taught his way of thinking nearly 2500 years ago, his beliefs were that 'whatever affects the mind affects the body'. This view was partially lost during the seventeenth century when western scientific thinking, led by Descartes, divided human beings into separate entities, a body and a mind.

The Greeks and Egyptians used hypnosis extensively, indeed, hypnosis is named using the Greek word for 'Sleep', 'hypnos'. This confusion with words is, where much of the misconceptions about hypnosis lie, as it is not really sleep as such. These sessions are widely regarded as an early form of hypnosis. The Bible has many references to 'magical happenings' that with today's hindsight can be attributed to forms of hypnotic phenomena and suggestion.

500 BC—Hellenistic Period. Documentation is quite specific as to the use of 'Sleep Temples' throughout the time of ancient civilisation. These temples would in most cases be prepared by Priests for the ill. The methods are easily compared to techniques used by physicians such as Sigmund Freud in his Psycho-analysis. Priests would interpret the patients dreams using suggestion, whilst they were resting in the sleep temples. Bad demons and spirits were consequently released and a cure would be found.

1733—Dr Franz Anton Mesmer developed 'animal magnetism' or 'mesmerism', which was later renamed hypnosis. One of the forefathers of hypnosis Mesmer was considered a bit of a rogue during his lifetime. Originally destined for the church Mesmer decided to follow his interest in Medicine and went to Vienna to study. His other interests in cosmology, religion, music and his friendship with Mozart all had influences in his medical work.

Mesmer viewed illness as a disharmony both within the human entity but also in external cosmic forces. Mesmer left Vienna in 1778 due partly to the hostile attitude towards him from the establishment. He set up practice in France. His life's work of Magnetism used hypnotic techniques and the influences of suggestion in it's ability to cure. Mesmer's ability to treat up to one hundred patients at a time and his success rate irritated the medical establishment, consequently by the end of his career Mesmerism was banned in France, and he decided to retire. Certainly he was taking huge amounts of income away from Medical Doctors, because of the high profile and large turn over of patients he was able to treat. Mesmerism continued to thrive by other practitioners using predominantly 'post hypnotic suggestion' and hypnosis to induce anaesthesia for surgery.

1795—1860—James Braid. James Braid was a Scottish eye doctor and physician. After witnessing Mesmerism demonstrating a somnambulistic state ('deep' hypnosis), Braid's scepticism encouraged him to investigate the patient. He did this by forcing a pin beneath the subjects nail, which had little effect upon the person. Braid was impressed and went on to complete many experiments. It was 1842 when Braid published his first book on Hypnosis, which is where he coined the term Hypnosis. In his form of hypnosis Braid used a shiny or bright object and instructed the patient to stare at it.

1845—1853—James Esdaile British surgeon and friend of Braid performed 2,000 operations including amputations with patients under Hypno-anaesthesia. Esdaile was said to cut the fatality rate of patients in major surgery from fifty percent down to five percent using Hypnosis. Consequently, Esdaile was the first person to convince the Medical Establishment of the benefits in the use of hypnosis and accept it as a useful tool.

19th Century—Hypnosis was found to be the most effect form of cure for human illness. It wasn't until the discovery of Chloroform that hypnosis was replaced, as the foremost treatment for painless surgery, perhaps a mistake that society may never recover from. This led the way for the medical industry to gain profit from the development of medicines and to discard any possible natural, less lucrative cure for disease. A phenomenon we still see today.

1853—Queen Victoria was administered Chloroform during childbirth. Subsequently chloroform replaced hypnosis as the favoured form of pain relief in Britain, just as the establishment was beginning to accept it.

1857-1926—Emile Coue pioneered the use of autosuggestion and positive affirmations, perhaps one of the best still widely used today; 'Everyday and in every way I am getting Better and Better'.

1849-1936—Ivan Petrovich Pavlov (1904 Nobel Prize winner), Russian physiologist known for his ground breaking work on 'conditional responses'. Pavlov argued that psychological processes are directly linked to physiological states in the brain. Classical conditioning is said to be a primitive, reflex process.

1856—1939 Sigmund Freud. Perhaps one of the most influential physicians of modern day mind therapies. Sigmund was the pioneer of 'Free-association' and to a smaller degree the use of Hypno-analysis. He went on to develop Psychoanalysis, due to a misunderstanding and subsequently mistrust of hypnosis. Later, some time just before his death Sigmund admitted that he may have been mistaken in his underestimation of hypnosis and thought perhaps it could be the answer that he had been looking for in unconscious behaviour.

1914—The First World War brought hypnosis back into medical use. The Germans used it as a way to dull pain during surgery when their levels of Chloroform ran down in the battlefields.

1938—The second world war saw a new wave of Hypnotherapy use not just for pain control but for the psychological treatment of War Trauma. Sir Winston Churchill is said to have used self-hypnosis to avoid tiredness during long nights in the war.

1958—The British Medical Association gave their seal of approval for the use of Hypnosis to their members, as long as they were 'suitably qualified'. This was the first time hypnosis had gained a legitimate approval from the medical establishment.

1968—The British Society of Medical and Dental Hypnosis was founded.

1901 to 1980—Milton H. Erickson MD, considered an authority on clinical and indirect hypnosis, was making huge breakthroughs in the creative use of hypnosis to cure a multitude of ailments. Many of his ideas used the findings of Ivan Pavlov's theories of unconscious conditioning and conditional reflex. Principally Erickson used unconscious behaviour and the alteration of 'states' to cure his patients.

1980—Out of 20 Australian swimmers named in the Olympic team 12 had been using Les Cunningham's hypnosis tapes for two months previously.—*'Hypnosport' by Les Cunningham.*

1993—New Scientist magazine published its results of the largest recorded survey ever, in smoking cessation. Hypnosis proved to be the most effective form of stopping smoking compared to any other method - world wide.

1996—Steve Collins beat Chris Eubank for the World Boxing Organisations Super-middleweight title. Much of his success being attributed to the focusing of attention created by hypnosis administered by Dr Tony Quinn, himself a former Champion bodybuilder. Collins was programmed to deliver two punches to Eubank's one. In the fight Eubank threw 300 punches, Collins threw over 600.

Nigel Benn, WBC Super Middleweight Champion and Frank Bruno, WBC Heavyweight Champion both used Sports hypnosis for Boxing performance enhancement, they were hypnotised by Paul Mckenna.

More recently Athlete Iwan Thomas and Golfer Ian Woosnam were hypnotised by Robert Farago.

Chapter Two

▼

THE MIND AND BODY CONNECTION
—*autogenic gymnastics.*

'The fact that the mind rules the body is, in spite of its neglect by biology and medicine, the most fundamental fact which we know about the process of life'.
—Franz Alexander, MD.

Mind Power—*the champions mental tool box.*

Psychology, Psychiatry, Psychotherapy, Hypnotherapy, Hypno-Analysis and any other science pertaining to the mind brings with it suspicion and often fear. All of the above are natural phenomena, there is no 'physical' interference such as in surgery. Surgery is used to 'cut out' the aftermath of a problem; it has arisen from the inability of humans to find the reasons behind physical problems. Surgery is the 'cure' for symptoms rather than the cure for the cause of the symptoms. This appears to be a short-term effect for a long-term problem. It's all very well cutting out a cancer tumour from a patient to stop the spread of the disease, but unless the cause of the problem is dealt with, then the cancer in all probability will return. I am not claiming that surgery does not have its benefits, it is essential in our society, however I do feel too much emphasis is put onto the cure of diseases and not enough time and money spent on preventing problems before they happen.

The mind therapies such as Psychiatry and Hypnosis are all techniques which use nothing but words and communication. So where does the fear of these sciences come from? Subconscious resistance is one problem, a problem that we will not go into too deeply in this text, for the primary reason that it has little value in the area of sports performance. Subconscious resistance has many varied reasons in mental health, some still unclear today. The general consensus of opinion is that the mind represses thoughts, emotions, feelings and experiences to the subconscious primarily to protect the 'young' mind from harm. When we grow into adult hood we are able to 'handle' experiences with a greater sense of understanding, therefore bad experiences are less likely to be repressed after teenage years. Having said this, experiences, which shock us to some degree such as car accidents, are often repressed at least in part for a short period. This can be demonstrated in the way accident victims often 'forget' the entire incident thus protecting them from the parts which are excessively distressing, such as situations with injuries involved. We know that these incidents are still in the psyche because of our experience with recall through hypnosis and the fact that many people find these events gradually 'coming back' to them at a conscious level after the incident.

Another reason for the irrational fear of therapies, and this is especially true in the context of hypnosis, is the fear of having ones 'power' taken away. We all like to think that we have our own minds, that no one can manipulate or control them, and certainly no one really knows what our own thoughts and feelings are. This is true to a certain degree. No-one knows what you or I think, and you don't know what others think. More importantly it's not really anyone's business to know, unless you decide to tell them. This said, human beings are surprisingly predictable in their behaviours and one can presuppose their actions with amazing accuracy, in many situations.

A huge element in the perception of mind control regarding hypnosis grows from those entertaining breeds that go by the name of 'Stage Hypnotists'. Some would claim that stage hypnotists do the image of hypnosis more harm than good. Personally I am divided between the two perceptions.

It's good that they create awareness for clinical hypnosis and some of the benefits it has, however the perceptions created by stage hypnosis sometimes generates fear and misunderstanding in the minds of the general public.

It is in the interest of the stage performer to give the illusion that what's happening to his hypnotised participant is magical and a little weird. The Hypnotist benefits greatly from the image that he is in total control, that all participants automatically do as he instructs under his will. You will find out later when you learn about hypnosis that this is in fact untrue, all subjects have total control over their minds and bodies. The subject is consciously or unconsciously giving their approval to the hypnotist's suggestions.

Suggestion is not a phenomenon that works only on the unconscious mind, its use can be just as effective at a conscious level. Countless experiments by psychologists and physiologists have proven that the human being can change his or her own beliefs significantly enough to alter the body in some astounding ways. Pain is eased or physical ailments cleared up in situations where drugs were unable to assist.

Milton H Erickson the renowned hypnotherapist conducted many experiments demonstrating the ability to control physiological functions.

'I don't think this subject should be taken too lightly. In the Laboratory I've seen a hypnotised subject with his hands in the plethysmogragh [a device for measuring blood flow] respond excellently to my instruction, "Make your right hand smaller and your left hand larger." Indeed, the blood vessels shrunk in one hand and dilated in the other. Now that seemed to be an excellent demonstration of the possibility of bringing about physiological changes by hypnotic measures. But when I actually questioned the subject, his reaction—his explanation was, " I can do that without being in a trance"; and he very neatly and carefully proceeded to demonstrate the same phenomenon. The man had a very, very vivid imagination. He would think about holding the ice and getting his hand very, very cold; and he would think about immersing the other hand in very warm water. Naturally he got his vasomotor dilation, and the hypnosis had nothing to do with it!'

Mind-Body Communication in Hypnosis. The Seminars,
Workshops and Lectures of Milton Erickson Volume 3.
Nonhypnotic Alterations in Physiological Functions Page 2.

The test carried out by Milton shows more than one phenomenon at work, the strongest being the development of the subjects own belief system, a side effect often encountered by the practising hypnotist. The subject in question did have the ability to alter his physiology before he met the hypnotherapist although it is unclear as to whether he was able to perform the feat of physiological change, this is impossible to tell in hindsight. The subject had his beliefs in his own abilities either confirmed or probably strengthened by performing an alteration under hypnosis. Consequently he realised or believed he could do this whilst out of trance. This turned out to be true. The question is did he have the strength of belief before he achieved it under hypnosis or did that cause the belief? This cannot be answered in retrospect, but it can be said that his neurology did not change. All human beings are capable of such physiological changes as long as they are able to develop belief systems strong enough to achieve this. Hypnosis is a superb way of achieving such belief systems because the 'doubting' conscious mind is to some extent 'reduced' in awareness thus a belief can be installed straight to the subconscious. This can be seen in some forms of mentally unstable people such as 'Multiple Personalities'* who have the ability to change their physiology in astounding ways. This is due to their immense certainty that they are a different person with different traits. It is documented that some people with Multiple Personality Disorders are able to change their own eye colour to coincide with the split in their personality.

It is possible to change ones own belief system. Many people have totally irrational perceptions of how the world is and their own view of themselves in it, both on a positive and negative scale.

Another strong argument for the hypnotic subject mentioned is his ability to visualise. Visualisation is a key element in hypnosis, in fact hypnosis is visualisation and vice versa. We all have the ability to visualise, if we did not we wouldn't be able to count for example, it is impossible to do sums without visualising the numbers or figures in someway. The varying degrees of our abilities to visualise does vary though. I believe we can develop our visualisation skills through practice. Many people have weak visualisation muscles, which could benefit from exercise. Artists and designers are people who have enhanced abilities as hypnotic subjects due to their well worked visualisation skills.

No one can say with clarity when it is that we are in one state of awareness to another state, due to the varying degrees within ourselves and the differences between individuals (although there are clear signs of hypnosis). The line drawn between the two is impossible to define with accuracy. It is similar to the concept as to whether an individual act has occurred in one way or another in our personal perceptions of reality. Any Police officer will tell you the differing accounts which witnesses give of the same event. Who is correct? It's all subjective. Is there a shadow behind you? Is a shadow real? You can't touch it but you can manipulate its shape? You cannot feel the texture of a shadow or hear its sound, but you can manipulate its shape and tone. What makes a shadow any more real than a thought? You cannot see thoughts but you can hear them in your own mind and you can measure and manipulate them. Does this make your thoughts objects; does it make them real? Are they tangible things? Who's to tell?

Are you feeling the emotion of anger or is it frustration? Who labelled that emotion for you? How do you know anger means the same to you as it does to someone else? You can never feel what they are feeling to compare the differences, you might have the labels mixed up!

To master your mind in the sporting arena all these types of questions should be considered, you must become aware of your internal dialogue and the reasons for your emotions. Only then can you change your behaviours to your benefit.

The mind and body became disassociated mainly by the medical profession who separated the two for ease of learning about the subjects. Although interrelated it makes the learning process far easier if one separates sections or chunks of information in to areas of interest. Medicine has standardised illnesses because of today's need to treat vast amounts of patients in small amounts of time. Individual treatment and care is diminishing in our society through lack of resources, which is one explanation for the huge rise in patients seeking 'complementary therapies'.

*Not to be confused with Schizophrenia
which is a split between thought and effect rather than personalities.

The Placebo Effect—*mind body power in action.*

'On average Placebos are 55 per cent as effective in pain relief as morphine.'
Evans, F. 'Expectancy, therapeutic instructions and the placebo response'
in White, L. B. and Schwarts, G. *Placebo:*
Theory, research and mechanism, Guildfold Press, 1985, p.215-28.

The word 'Placebo' is Latin for 'I will please'. The Placebo effect is a widely known condition used by almost every pharmacological and medical establishment on this planet to decipher the 'real' and 'imaginary' effects of drugs and substances upon humans. A placebo is a preparation often used in controlled conditions whilst testing the differences between the pharmacological and psychological effects of a drug. In a doctor/patient situation the patient's expectations of the placebo are a key element in the cure of a disease. In other words, if your doctor prescribed you a sugar pill and insisted it was in fact a powerful headache pill, it is very likely that your headache would subside rapidly, due only to the psychological affects delivered by yourself.

This occurs all the time. Some hypnosis associations have a percentage of their members who are practising Dentists, and these dentists use such effects almost on a daily basis. Many medical practitioners are of the mind that drugs should be administered as a last resort only, which is a very commendable opinion. Due to this mentality they may take it on themselves to 'trick' their patients into believing in a placebo effect for their own health and well being. An example might be when the dentist is about to pull a tooth. It has been known that the dentist will rub a swab of cool numbing solution onto the tooth until complete feeling is lost. The dentist will suggest that this liquid will numb the tooth from pain, in actual fact he used very cold water instead of any drug at all. It is usually the case that the patient will react positively to the suggestion of the trusted practitioner and anaesthetise their own tooth through the power of their mind and belief systems. Consequently no pain is felt, due totally to the patient's personal power.

These effects are very powerful. In many cases placebo's bring with them side effects of the given deception drug. Even though the medication was nothing but a sugar pill, the person's beliefs created both a cure and the side effects of a totally separate and absent drug.

Surgeons separated the mind and body for ease of explanation. Modern day 'mind doctors' such as psychiatrists increase this perception. It is much easier to explain certain actions by separation of mind and body, but we need to remember everything that a person does is initiated in the mind. Only then can we begin to grasp the extent of our abilities and performances. One popular view today is the holistic view that we are a 'whole' or 'oneness'. This sometimes goes a little further by the addition of spiritual life and a oneness with earth. If we break down the human body to a cellular level structurally there is little difference between the human being and a wooden table or chair. This is where the argument originates that we are all directly related in a oneness with the earth and its contents.

Having defined a placebo as a drug like substance in the above text, it was for demonstration purposes only. In fact a placebo can be anything that changes a persons expectations in a way that focuses their belief systems having an effect upon their physiology. In ancient times witch doctors stuck needles in Voodoo dolls and directed them at an unfortunate individual. Voodoo religious practices use forms of affirmations and visualisation closely related to hypnosis. The effect would be a painful death, even though there was no reason for the subject to die other than an immensely strong belief in the consequences of such a ritual. This is the very power of suggestion that a Placebo inflicts, whether consciously or not.

Belief Systems—*the foundations of excellence.*

'Whatever the mind can conceive and believe, it can achieve'.
—Napoleon Hill,
Think and Grow Rich—Wiltshire book company.

Belief systems are the essence of human behaviour, they create our personalities, they direct what we aim for in life, and whether we achieve it. When you have enough references in your experience to build a rock solid belief system you always get a positive outcome. Alternatively you can direct your mental energies to create an imaginary series of experiences that will give you exceptional results, through hypnosis and affirmations.

Let me give you an example of the power of belief systems. An exciting example would be Roger Bannister back in 1954. He's at the starting line ready to run an attempt at the 'four minute mile'! The crowd is excited and eager for the record to be broken, but in reality they know it is unlikely, no one has done it before, it can't be done. Roger is a man who had incredible mind power, he knew how to use mental imagery to gain positive results in his life. I am sure that Roger had run the four-minute mile hundreds of times before in his mind, long before he physically did it. He had the positive belief systems to know without a shadow of doubt that he could beat the record.

The record had been attempted unsuccessfully many times before, for years this was the record to break, but to no avail. Roger Bannister became the first to beat this record.

The most interesting aspect of this story is that when Bannister eventually succeeded there came an influx of successful attempts. One after another countless athletes broke the four minute mile. Over 30 runners broke the four minute mile in the year after Roger did it. So what had happened? Did they all gain physiological changes that enabled them to run faster? No they did not. Did they all find a new running technique and shared it amongst themselves, which enhanced their performance? No, none of these are true. The reason so many people could now beat the old record was that they now knew it was possible. Each person could represent in his or her own mind beating the clock, they had a new internal representation. Bannister had not only empowered himself but hundreds of other people to change their belief systems. He had helped create strong beliefs in other athletes minds so that for them too this was possible.

This is an example of how the human body is capable of the most exceptional feats if the belief system is strong enough.

The sporting arena is awash with great examples of the power of beliefs and suggestion.

You are warming up on the Rugby pitch and your opponents come running on. To your dismay they all tower over you and weigh a good two stones heavier! Now, you have a choice on what you communicate to yourself in your own mind. The internal dialogue for a less than experienced athlete is to communicate to their nervous system 'Oh no, we're going to get battered, they are going to pound us'! Usually this becomes a self-fulfilling prophecy. A much better example might be to focus on the weaknesses of these people. If they are much larger in size, perhaps tell yourself that they will be too big and slow to be effective against you.

This is a technique I picked up in boxing and still use today both with clients and in areas of my life where I feel I need extra abilities. Focusing on your own strengths and the opponent's weaknesses can communicate to your subconscious that you are better and ultimately worthy of success.

Let me show you an example of this from a personal sports experience in the area of competitive Boxing. When you come across an opponent who looks bigger and more muscular, someone who in reality might be much stronger than yourself, you would use your internal dialogue to ridicule him, and put him down on his perceived weaknesses. This has two effects, one is to give you and your body the confidence to win and two to relax you and take some of the stress away so that you'd focus more easily on the task at hand. When this larger opponent approached you would justify 'he's going to be so slow being so big' 'I'm going to run rings around him, there is no way this man can possibly keep up with me, I'm slimmer, quicker, more agile'! This type of positive focusing encourages one to realise there are gaps in every athletes armoury. It also serves to cut out the inevitable negative self-talk that pops-up when fear and tension present themselves. There is always a positive side to view any situation, begin first to view it in a creative manner, this will elevate your thoughts and feelings.

At the other end of the scale if your opponent turns up smaller and perhaps faster, you could justify that he would be too weak to hurt you, 'I'm much bigger and stronger, I'm going to knock him out easily'. As you can see it doesn't really matter how well one of your opponents turn out. It doesn't matter how fit, how strong, how quick, how experienced. You focus on their weaknesses, not their strengths. More importantly you'd focus in such a way that you'd feel you had strength related to them, this gives an unconscious signal to your nervous system that success is yours. There is still a need to be objective, never under estimate an opponent, and have confidence in your abilities.

This technique can work with any sport. Try thinking up some images for a scenario that may occur in your sport so you can have them ready to saturate your mind at a competition. Be sure to create emotion when you say them to yourself. Get excited by the fact that you've noticed how you can beat the opposition. Believe it. If your opponent is much more experienced than you are, do not use this to fall apart during competition. This can be seen at competitions where belts are worn to suggest experience. The Martial Arts are an example. If you are a relative novice and you get through to a bout where you end up against say, a black belt, realise the advantages in this. The black belt is sure to be a little complacent coming up against a lower grade opponent. There are many ways that you now have the opportunity to catch this experienced competitor off guard. Do something he does not expect from a novice, ask your coach for tips, you have the advantage here of surprise. I know some sports people use this technique to gain advantage. They deliberately resist taking extra grades so that their belt does not reflect their talent. This way opponents under estimate their abilities.

These are all good examples of how one can gain control of emotions through the focus of attention. When looked at in more detail it becomes clear that these are merely ways of changing how we feel thus accessing different states of mind or arousal levels. In the sporting arena champions often do this at an unconscious level. The cyclist will hypnotise himself by focusing on the rhythmic swishing sounds of his tyres on tarmac and the regular inhaling and exhale of his breath. He'll visualise his thighs as powerful mechanical pistons that have an endless momentum.

The Tennis player might 'shift from foot to foot' using up nervous energy swaying themselves into a calm, relaxed sense of body whilst keeping the mind alert, ready to receive the next serve.

The Will—*gaining inner strength to push your body to its limits.*

'You just can't beat the person who never gives up'
Babe Ruth, 1895-1948,
World Record Breaking Baseball player.

Muscles only have a pulling action; no muscle pushes a limb. A forearm is moved upwards by the Bicep muscles pulling on the limb and moved back again by the Triceps pulling in the other direction. This accounts for the perception of the hypnotised person seen in stage acts who with the greatest of will finds it impossible to lift a one gram pencil for example. The suggestion would have been made that the pencil will feel as if it weighed as much as a tonne. The physiology behind this will be that the subject will exert more 'pulling' power upon their tricep muscles than on the opposing bicep muscles which are trying to lift the pencil by pulling the forearm in an upward direction. This has the effect that the biceps feel an immense force against their power and the perception consciously that the pencil is extremely heavy. The subject will be none the wiser after the task is completed that their own muscles were working against each other.

Will power is the crux of any endurance or stamina based sport and it is controlled predominantly by visualisation and what you choose to focus upon.

As we will see later, hypnosis is a visualisation based science. When we strengthen the 'Will' by hypnosis we can push our sporting performances far beyond what we usually achieve. If one can use the imagination to dominate the will, an athlete's muscles can be pushed to their limits.

The imagination is the key to continued endurance of muscle contraction. Often the mind will give up before the muscle needs to. Pain will be felt due to lactic acid build up, but you can still push through and continue with the exercise if there is sufficient motivation. Studies have shown that using hypnotic scripts that inspire the athlete into action (such as some sort of danger response) the athlete far exceeds his potential, often doubling output due to the new form of motivation.

All of this said, it must be realised that muscles need warming up substantially before a force is exerted. If not warmed up muscles and tendons break before the bone reaches its peak. An example can be found by the many arm wrestlers who frequently break each other's wrists and forearms during competition. Their strength of mind and the force put upon the arm outweighs the strength of the bone resulting in a break. The muscles had been directed to continue flexing beyond the strength of the bone.

Goal setting—*the elite athletes mental microscope.*

'Even if you are on the right track, you will get run over if you just sit there.'
—Will Rogers.

Time goals are helpful up to a point however we must remain aware that humans are unable to predict the future to an exact degree. We can only help to steer the results we achieve. Some aspects in the world are totally out of our control. Setting time frames for our goals is important, as long as they remain flexible. Concern for reaching the goal in the given time zone should not be overly important. The goals attainment is the crucial element, not the time frame in which it is achieved. If the time frame is missed, reassess the goal and continue in its direction until reached.

Many aspects in both sports and hypnosis are related to focusing of attention or concentration. Concentration implies that there is an 'object' to focus upon. An object in this sense can mean a real or imaginary target, it might be a vision, dream or specific bodyweight or condition. This is the essence to goal setting, focus on a target and you increase the likelihood of its attainment dramatically. Everyone needs this blueprint to their future, it sets a course of action, and enables one to achieve consistent results rather than sporadic ones.

Planning goals need not be overly complicated. If you write down your goals on a single sheet of paper, this at least is good enough to get some sort of direction. Of course if you can create emotion attached to these goals they become inspiring forms of motivation, helping you to get to the gym.

An important aspect of goal setting is most evident in bodybuilding circles. Bodybuilders often find themselves counting repetitions when training, this can be useful in monitoring their progress but also disruptive when each rep becomes a focal point. As I have mentioned, time lines are often overly emphasised in sporting goals, but the same process can be seen in this repetition counting attitude. In bodybuilding and other sports, it is important to be aware of your bodily sensations, concentrating upon repetitions mis-directs this focus. Use your goal setting wisely but remain flexible in your approach, if one aspect is not achieving the desired result change it. A well known phenomenon in the personal development industry is that wherever we are in our lives today, is not where we will be in the future. The behaviours that got us here will need to change to get us somewhere different tomorrow. Nothing in life stands still, you are either progressing or regressing. This clearly states that you need to view life and in particular goal setting as a form of personal evolution. A form of organic growth; ever changing to your environment and situation. Goals need to be flexible enough to meet the ever changing demands of life, those aspects that we are unable to manipulate. Use goals to set your course, but review them regularly.

Alan, 100 metre Sprinter—case study 1.

Alan was an amateur one hundred metre sprinter, already quite accomplished in his field and a bit of a celebrity in his own right. Charismatic and well liked in the athletics circuit. He was relaxed and had a nice level of dedication to his sport but lacked abilities to understand his own style faults and motivations.

Alan was sent to me by his athletic coach who was well aware of Alan's performance faults. He had been unable to correct them to the degree that was required. Alan's coach had tried everything but to no avail, Alan had kept on trying harder and harder increasing his practice times until he had come to this point where he was unable to give any more time to the pursuit.

I discovered from our initial discussion with Alan's coach that he had a good sprint style and trained hard, but it was clear that his performance would dramatically elevate if only he reacted more quickly to the starting gun. Alan had a habit of either 'jumping' the gun or under reacting and losing vital seconds. A quick start is essential to the short distance runner.

The ability of hypnosis to work upon the subconscious mind gives the possibility of programming unconscious behaviour traits quickly. I was aware that if I worked with Alan to develop unconscious 'triggers' it would enable him to react much more rapidly to given stimuli, in this case the starter gun.

The reaction to a starter gun is gradually developed into an unconscious behaviour through repetition of conscious activity that the athlete partakes in. In theory any task practised continuously will eventually become an unconscious behaviour, *this is called learning!* The problem arises when practice is not perfect. If the athlete makes mistakes in practice he develops more than one pathway to his desired result, therefore more than one outcome is possible. In competition the athlete opens up the possibility of using his winning formula, or the behaviour that creates a non-satisfactory result.

This is one reason why coaches recommend visualisation as an important training aid. There is the option of always getting it right when rehearsing in the mind therefore reinforcing the winning formula rather than the poor performance. Visualisations ability to communicate desires to the nervous system is almost as effective as completing the task in the real world. The results of visualisation at a cellular level are dramatically similar, muscle fibres contract, enhanced healing occurs and cells duplicate when directed to.

Our work began in my consultation room. Using visualisation aided by hypnosis, and including all the sounds, smells emotions and feelings Alan would have experienced at race day. I gave suggestions that he would almost foresee the sound of the starter gun before it reached his ears, giving him acute hearing and lightening quick reactions. Although Alan had the perception that he was able to foresee the sound of the gun, we made sure he 'waited' for the sound to leave the gun, it was important that he did not practice false starts.

Further suggestions were made that Alan was able to switch on his senses to the starting gun. This would mean hearing the trigger, feeling the vibrations of the noise, even the smell of ignition. Other sensory experiences were less important in his attention, I didn't want Alan to start a heightened awareness to noises in the crowd for instance.

Heightened awareness of the senses, as we will discover later, is indeed a phenomenon of hypnosis. These suggestions were received willingly and belief was heightened because under hypnosis, Alan did experience these sensations as I mentioned them.

An aspect that I focused upon, but in a somewhat smaller degree was Alan's tendency to slow down very slightly at the end of the one hundred metres mark. You will notice this to be a common trait amongst track athletes; they over excel and begin to slow down within of a few feet of the finishing line. This can mean the difference between winning or losing or the attainment of a record or not.

The combination of these two key elements in Alan's performance were phenomenal. Alan managed to shave off nearly half a second in his 100 hundred metres time, for a track athlete at his level this was remarkable. The main aspects of our work together was to set a 'trigger' (the gun) to a level of arousal and a behaviour (out of the blocks).

Now our work together has finished Alan still uses the techniques that I taught him to increase his focus and visualise the performance results and style that he wants to achieve.

Chapter Three

Internal Dialogue
—the linguistic nutrition of champions.

'Champions aren't made in the gym. Champions are made from something they have deep inside them—a desire, a dream, a vision. They have to have last-minute stamina, they have to be a little faster, they have to have skill and the will. But the will has to be stronger than the skill'

—Mohammed Ali.

Positive thoughts—*athletic blueprint to success.*

Flooding your mind with positive thoughts and suggestions will communicate to the unconscious mind the result you require—a win!

The unconscious mind knows no logic. If you consistently direct it, to win or to lose you will receive that result. It creates a self-fulfilling prophecy. A fear of success or a fear of failure can have the same result—a loss!

It is widely recognised that our internal dialogue is predetermined by our parents and those influential to us during our early days, at around the age of four years old.

The negative suggestions often intended to be positive have an effect of setting our psyches up for life. The parents usually have only good intentions, telling a child off for approaching some kind of danger, is seen as a positive thing. Perhaps in some cases an emphasis on praise and encouragement should be a replacement for the more common 'telling off' scenario which research suggests has a negative effect later on in life. Clearly we are unable to change our pasts, and it could be seen to be mentally unhealthy to dwell on past experiences. Focusing on the present and those aspects that we can change in our lives for the better is a far more desirable and exciting prospect.

We have already discussed belief systems and the profound effects they can have upon the sporting person. In this Chapter we will focus on the internal dialogue of the individual. This is both the foundation of creating a more effective belief system, and a tool that will help you change the way you feel and harness your emotions. In this way you will learn to begin to cut out negative, destructive forces from your internal and external environments.

Every human being has an internal and external world to a greater or lesser degree. We all talk to ourselves inside our minds. We mull over bad experiences, praise ourselves after a good result, or tell ourselves how sexy we look whilst looking in the mirror in the morning! Whatever the occasion, I like to call this ' internal dialogue', dialogue within our own minds (some might say that 'internal monologue' would be a more appropriate term, however my view is that most of our self-talk is in the form of questions and answers, therefore I favour 'dialogue'). We all have this natural dialogue. This is different from the mentally unhealthy state of a Schizophrenic who hears dissociated voices that he feels he has no connection with. These are still his own thoughts or self-talk but he fails to view it in that way.

When trying to change any part of your life, the quality of internal dialogue is the key aspect to fast and effective change. Becoming aware of our dialogue and manipulating it to our advantage is a simple process to make. It is easy. The only real challenge is catching negative thoughts and feelings as soon as they occur then restricting them for the better.

Controlling the inner dialogue is the main attribute to increasing self-esteem and a host of other personal development issues, which certainly does not exclude athletic performance.

The self-manipulation of our internal dialogue is closely related to our internalisation of our success or failure in sports. Locus of Control is the term used in social psychology that refers to a persons perceived source of behaviour control and the cause of life's events. There are two general extremes, those who view themselves as having control over their life events (Internal) and those who blame external fate and forces such as destiny or society for the control over their lives (External). The most important term in this area is 'perception'. It is the persons perception not 'reality' that distinguishes between the two viewpoints.

In sports this 'locus of control' theory is most apparent when focusing upon the perception of ones opponents abilities and the general athletic environment.

Locus of control varies from one person to another and it is unlikely that any given person will have one extreme or another, probably a mixture of the two. It is also true that we tend to show different variants in different situations, our perceptions of control change depending upon the situation encountered. For instance one person may blame all their financial worries on the present government but their sporting achievements upon themselves entirely.

The good news is that we are consciously able to change these perceptions of control to suit our expectations. The athlete might attribute a past failure on excessive external forces which he or she was unable to control. Bad track conditions might be a good example of external blame that has the effect of saving the athletes confidence to compete again in the future. Although it is nice to blame failure on external sources, one should remain level headed. Increasing confidence is good, but taking a total lack of responsibility will have a detrimental effect on future performances. When things go wrong one needs to focus on possible shortcomings and to make adjustments.

Highly motivated athletes often adopt a high level of internal control to success; they take credit for their competitive wins. The main point here is that it's mentally healthy for the athlete to internalise success as long as they still take some responsibility for their own actions. However the internalisation of failure can result in lack of future motivation, frustration and a low level of self-esteem. A point we need to remember is that reality is not the issue in our source of locus of control, reality is frequently difficult to alter but our perceptions are not. If somebody is making excessive noise in the gym we have a choice on how to react to that situation and how we focus on those issues. You may not be able to control the noise, but you can take charge of your own internal environment. You might decide to take a personal stereo to the gym in the future.

Self-Sabotage
—*reducing the fear of suffering what you fear!*

'A Champion is afraid of losing. Everyone else is afraid of winning.'
—Billie Jean King. 1943
—Six times Wimbledon singles champion.
US Tennis Champion 4 times.

Self-sabotage is surprisingly a much greater element in the cause of failure than one would commonly expect. Research psychologists now suggest that many people are less successful than they would wish to be. Mainly due to their own actions not the environment or even circumstances. It is also suggested that a key to the management of our goals is perhaps not so much in the focus of why we are not succeeding in the acquisition of our desires, but why are we failing?

It must be noted that this sabotage of ones own success is not delivered at a conscious level but an unconscious one. Certainly it can be said to be true that the majority of people really do want and strive for success. No one likes the pain of failure (although some enjoy the attention they gain from failure).

The key then to this form of success sabotage is to realise that there is a pattern emerging of constant failure and perhaps more importantly what are ones true values and goals in life? People's values are often in conflict and this is one reason why they destroy the personal process of success.

The smoker might be a good example. Smokers often want to give up, they know the huge risks involved in smoking, but still they fail to discontinue their habit. Smokers believe that they smoke because it makes them feel relaxed and thus cheers them up. They also claim that they enjoy it and the taste of burnt tar as well! In reality this is totally untrue. Not a single soul on this earth enjoys the taste of tar and smoke, no matter how much they convince themselves or others that they do. It's also a fact that smoking does not relax the body, it increases blood pressure and causes anxiety. The only reason smokers feel they are more relaxed when smoking is their excessively high levels of nicotine in the blood. They already have high blood pressure and anxiety. Now when that person has a break from the cigarette, it could be any amount of time depending on the size of the habit, this is when the level of nicotine starts to reduce in the blood and even more anxiety is experienced. Another cigarette is administered and the anxiety levels drop down again to the original (already high) level. This gives the impression that the stress level of the smoker is being reduced.

What we can see from this example is that a smoker may feel that their main aim is to give up smoking, for whatever reason, usually the health benefits. Trying to give up smoking for health reasons can be a difficult task when the smoker believes that he/she is benefiting from a reduced stress level from nicotine. The real benefit in this case is to reduce stress, or to become more relaxed. The focus and motivation in giving up smoking is not necessarily the benefit in health, but the cause of the stress in ones life. So the individuals wish is not to give up smoking but to reduce their stress levels. Granted this will inevitably mean giving up smoking as well, but the point is that when our values are established we can focus on one task at a time or re-evaluate our goals into a hierarchy of importance.

Another frequently seen form of success sabotage is the fear of consistency in success. An athlete is often afraid that if they reach a desired standard, perhaps to win at a National level, then they will be expected to continue winning at this level or to exceed it in the future.

The fear and pressure put on themselves to keep their performance at a consistent level can have a dramatic effect upon success. Often well meaning friends, family and coaches only act to enhance this fear, by talking and encouraging the athlete to look at the possibilities of future success.

The first step then for such a scenario is to accept that one has this fear and secondly to realise that this might well be expected of you. The people close to you do indeed enjoy your success and people like being associated with a winner. The truth is that you do not need to feel pressurised by these people. You need to take charge of your own feelings and decide what you are going to focus on. There is no real need to keep succeeding at a top level if that is not your main motivation. An effective answer to releasing some of this pressure is to tell your peers that their well meaning comments are affecting you, and your performance will increase if there is less pressure for you to perform. Ask them not to pressurise in this way, tell them that you will do your best, and this means being in a relaxed state with the pressures off.

Focusing attention on a specific goal is one of the best ways to cut out outside influences whatever they are.

In the past, I have had the privilege of training with a former ABA Heavyweight champion who also attended one of the Universities where I studied. He told of how he would cease going to his lectures or do any work whatsoever at University during the week running up to a fight. He would concentrate for a whole week, eating, visualising and preparing to win, focusing on nothing other than the fight. This gives an excellent example of how he used a form of hypnosis, although he didn't know it. It also shows that preparation is a superb ally to successful performance. This Boxer would clear up any work or tasks that he had to do at least a week before a fight, that way he had no outside pressure other than preparing for the bout. This left him time to focus and visualise on his skills and techniques needed to win, what we know as self-hypnosis. I challenge anyone to fail at succeeding using these techniques.

Sometimes we find benefits in not changing negative thoughts and feelings. The benefits in keeping destructive thoughts seem more comfortable than changing them to positive ones. In some cases we prefer to dwell on negative thoughts for some time to accomplish a secondary gain. And this can be a powerful barrier to positive change. Certainly it is not uncommon to meet people who seem to benefit greatly from feeling and acting depressed, and increasing this emotion through destructive internal dialogue has a strong secondary gain thus perpetuating the process.

Usually people can be seen to gain secondary benefits from being depressed or acting in someway where they might enjoy an increased amount of attention from friends and relatives. Often this is at an unconscious level and it is only when the subject becomes consciously aware of the process that they can begin to harness their emotions through self-talk.

Fear of Success can generate (unconsciously) obstacles to your goals. For example many people make excuses not to go to the gym, there always seems to be an obstacle in the way. Just finish this, just do that, and by the time the task is completed it's too late. Or 'oh I'm a bit tired today I'll go tomorrow.' Tomorrow never comes. Not only does this attitude prevent results due to the absence of a regular, structured training routine, but it also causes anxiety and stress as there are usually negative emotions associated with failing to train. The person would like to train but has not the motivation to get up and follow through. One answer I have found with clients and myself is to draw up a chart of days and times when you will go to the gym or train in some way. Then stick to it no matter what occurs. Trying not to think whether you will go or not, instead regard it as 'set in stone' miss that programme on television or video it! It's when the internal dialogue starts making excuses that you eventually find a viable one. Don't let it start.

Another useful tool to aid motivation is to create vivid mental images in your mind of the benefits and the reasons why you wish to train. Think of the body you will have, the admiration from friends of your achievements. Think of the competition that you will win or whatever it is that drives you. Make these images real and get excited!

The athlete must develop an awareness of their personal motivations. It might be the case that you have a 'negative' form of motivation that drives you to excellence, perhaps you are looking to prove yourself to peers. Sometimes the secondary gains achieved can be quite positive. If one competes in a sporting activity for the attention it brings it might be the case that excelling in the sport brings them more and more attention motivating them to gain an increasing amount of recognition. This can be achieved by winning.

In the same way people are often motivated through negative thoughts. 'Success is the greatest revenge' someone once said. Many athletes have found that a childhood experience of failure or mockery has driven them to high levels of achievement throughout their life. This can be seen in many successful entrepreneurs too. It's the 'rags to riches' story, where successful businessmen make a fortune after dropping out of school at an early stage. They use some reference to their past failure increasing their motivation to prove themselves to the mocking teachers or pupils. Perhaps not the most mentally healthy form of motivation but certainly very powerful and effective if used correctly. Communicating internally the notions of revenge through personal success can create strong emotional reactions, and as long as they are contained and directed to positive outcomes I feel they are not too harmful. The main concern with this form of motivation might be the possibility of a build up of emotions transferring into some sort of negative outward expression. If you can focus the negative energy on a positive sporting activity and attain the accomplishment through that endeavour there can be few problems. However negative thought is negative thought, so the possibility of realising ones motivation and re-focusing the energies in a new form may well result in an immense upturn in accomplishment. Not to mention the increased mental and physical health.

Many Boxers use this type of revenge motivation, although they do have a positive outlet for their pent up aggression that results from this internal dialogue. There are several reasons for a professional boxer to insult his opponent in days before their bout. One might be to out psyche the opponent, another is to create anger in the opponent thus making the boxer less technically balanced for a fight, using revenge in this sense is counter productive. As we know the calmer one remains the better one is to judge and act in a deliberate and skilful manner rather than blundering round full of high levels of adrenaline. The over aggressive boxer becomes sloppy and makes mistakes. This is all down to levels of arousal in sport. When we talk about levels of arousal we are essentially looking at emotions and the way in which we can consciously control them rather than react to them in an unconscious submissive manner. All of our emotions are biochemical waves in our brains, often triggered by unconscious external stimulus. As we discovered in Chapter One, when we discussed the mind body connection, our bodies are a single unit. The mind, body, emotions and physiological state are all inter-related, none of these can be truly separated.

We can see examples of reactive states in situations where one might have a phobic response when confronted with a perceived danger to a given stimuli. Often in our western society it is not the case that we need to consciously fear many situations. However once an unconscious response is programmed it is difficult for some people to act positively, even when they are intellectually aware of their unreasonable behaviour.

Fear Management—*sympathetic power reactors.*

> *'Courage is not the absence of fear; it is the making of action in spite of fear, the moving out against the resistance engendered by fear into the unknown and into the future'.*
>
> —M. Scott Peck—'The Road Less Travelled'.

An alternative approach to fear control is to behave in an opposite manner of what your fearful self-talk communicates to you. For instance if you were fearful of an up and coming event and found your internal voice creating excuses to justify a poor performance in the future, you might be saying 'best if I don't go to the gym today, looks like it going to start raining'. Then the approach would be to stop this dialogue and do exactly the opposite to this fear, you would get up and you'd indeed go out to the gym. Although simplified this is an example of the 'behavioural' approach often used for the treatment of Phobias. The approach works on the basis that if we face our fears consistently and progressively they subside. It is also true that fear will reach a plateau and then begin to diminish. A person reaches a high level of fear to a given stimuli with symptoms such as trembling limbs, excessive perspiration, increased heart rate, adrenaline release and increased blood pressure, then the fear has to diminish. Once this is realised you can accept the responses that you will have in the fearful situation, and then 'ride the storm' until things get better.

It is far easier to deal with a situation if you are aware of what will happen and that things can only get so bad until they improve again. Remember if you do fear a situation, you can always visit it first in a disassociated state through the power of visualisation.

Both in sport and life generally fear is experienced at different levels. These range from intense phobic responses to mental blocks in athletic performance.

It's often the case that injured sports people develop a phobic response to particular situations, for fear of incurring a similar injury in the future. An injured football player might think twice about diving feet first into a tackle in the aftermath of an injury incurred in such a situation. These fears are mental blocks based in the emotional right side of the brain; the side hypnosis has its main effect. The fears are irrational in a sense, because the injury is cleared up physically, otherwise the player's coach and physio would forbid playing. Also the likelihood of similar injuries occurring is statistically remote.

The emotions run wild, and a fear is developed predominately by the over active imagination, which as we've seen usually wins over the intellect. This is the point where hypnosis rears its head. Imagining the fearful scenario in a trance has the effect of role playing the sporting accomplishment without the fear involved.

One can imagine any situation, with any outcome and slow the process down to a snails pace thus making sure technique is correct. Often in practice it is difficult to slow the process down because gravity has its effect. In a golfing swing momentum is required to get the club to act in the correct way and in extreme sports such as cliff jumping it is somewhat difficult to slow down real life practice!

Results will be seen by visualisation in trance or out of trance, but trance visualisation proves to be far more vivid and effective, sending very clear signals to the nervous system of the required results. Remember the unconscious has no logic, it acts upon consistent directions. In hypnosis such is the realism of visualisation releases of adrenaline and other natural chemicals are the result. We've all experienced how vivid a nightmare can seem, physical reactions such as perspiration, increased heart rate and blood pressure are all symptoms suffered from mere imaginary scenarios.

In-trance visualisations can be just as effective in creating physiological effects.

Arousal Levels—*change your state, unleash performance results.*

'It's better to have lived one day as a Tiger, than one thousand years as a sheep.'
—Tibetan proverb.

In both life and sports your ability to alter your 'state' is the key to how you perform. If you have performed well in a particular situation you can do it again. The answer is to access the same level of arousal that you enjoyed the time before.

Everyone knows that an excess of bad stress can hinder athletic performance, the reason is clearly the altered emotional state this situation can bring. The better one becomes at controlling these emotional occurrences the better one can perform in any circumstance. A relatively well known account of this is in the case of the World Champion Bodybuilder turned film star Arnold Schwarzenegger. He recounts the time when his father died in Austria and the funeral coincided with his Mr Olympia Bodybuilding competition. Arnold was so focused and well adept at altering his level of arousal, he was able to regain his focus on the event. Arnold justified that there was little point returning to his family, as his father was already dead. This caused family disputes but Arnold cut these from his mind and continued to go on and win the title again. This is the immense power of the mind to control and manipulate the emotions at a conscious level.

You notice how powerfully you can direct your own mind once a strong enough motivation is found to focus on the task at hand.

The difference between a good sports performance and a bad one is the level of emotional arousal. Arousal is directly related to our physiology and internal dialogue.

Is it possible that you could access the state of depression or unhappiness if required? Most people can rapidly do this by thinking of some sort of failure in their life, a person they dislike or the way in which they felt when a partner left them. It's sometimes easy to gain access to undesirable emotions but apparently not so easy to access positive ones. It's just the same in the opposite direction, you can feel happy for no reason, you can make reasons to become excited, you can choose to be in any mood if you wish, just by focusing on those key aspects of the desired emotion.

There are many techniques to assist you in reaching emotional states quickly, ones you can learn to use very efficiently. Sports performance is no exception, there are times when one feels more powerful, full of energy or ready and motivated to go to the gym, even though it's cold and raining out side.

When you are in a negative state, such as being depressed, notice two main attributes; One is the things that you are focusing upon internally. What is it that you are saying to yourself in your own mind? Are you focusing on the things that you don't have, things that have gone wrong, rather than what's good, the parts you are happy with?

Depression has the ability to constrain the imagination, so one finds it difficult to focus on aspects other than the immediate problem. If this is a problem you need to break this cycle.

The second point is actual physical posture. Have you ever looked at a depressed person, or someone who is remembering a past athletic performance that did not go to their satisfaction? Notice the slumped shoulders, dropped head, eyes looking low.

You can change this state quickly in yourself and others. Lift the head high, look up, and pull the shoulders back, stand tall. That's the posture of confidence. Try feeling depressed standing in this way! You have to immediately access a new level of arousal; your body reacts to the signals right down to your nervous system.

In your athletic performance notice how you were positioned, your posture, and your internal dialogue everytime you achieve a good result.

Learn to revisit these levels to consistently access them when required. It's easy when you start to make the effort to notice them.

Ten Steps to Adjusting Arousal Levels in Sport.

The following list suggests ways to adjust arousal levels both at an increased and decreased rate. A decrease in arousal (low level) being similar to relaxation. This means the more complex a sport the lower the level of arousal required-and vice versa.

1. Increase or decrease rate of breathing, this will give a strong signal to your nervous system. There are many physiological reasons why slow, deep breathing through the nose exhibits a relaxed level of body and mind.

2. Focus by visualising your outcome. Imagine how you are going to feel whilst completing the task. How will your body feel during the performance? How will it feel during the outcome?

3. Release nervous energy by moving the muscles before the activity. You will often need to do this as a warm up anyway.

4. Use pre-planned associations to create visual images. What gets you excited? Visualise an event in your mind that inspires you with confidence or which ever emotion you are trying to create.

5. Use non realistic images if required. Mechanical, Powerful, Pistons for Leg muscles if you are about to sprint one hundred metres perhaps. Use your imagination, make it vivid, and personal. You might be as strong as a bear, or elegant as a dolphin in the water. Whichever sport, whatever the occasion, dream, make it feel real, remember your mind body connection has no logic or limitations.

6. Use process affirmations. Key words that inspire you, 'Easy', 'One more rep', 'No problem', 'Yes', 'Now', 'Power', 'Good', 'Come on', 'Do it', 'Winner', 'Energy', 'Blast' Etc... Construct words that are powerful and personal to you, words and phrases that create states

that you need to achieve at different points in your performance. By using a 'key word' at specific times of arousal during training, you will set-up basic 'Pavalovian' conditioning which is at the foundations of behavioural psychology. *(The original studies by Ivan Pavalov centred around the conditioned response in dogs. When a bell was rung and food administered to the dogs a neuro link was established which had the effect of making the dogs salivate. Later when only the bell was rung and no food was administered the dogs still salivated. The dogs made links with the tone and sound of the bell and their meal time. This basic unconscious response is also the key to human behaviour, such as phobic responses.)*

7. Go inside and imagine a time when you have been successful in a similar situation. Access that state, remember how it feels, this will enable you to reproduce that state once again.
8. Use props such as music to help access levels consistently.
9. Enjoy the feelings of nervousness—laugh about it. If you realise its an essential part of growing in life, it is far easier to cope with and can become fun. Rename nervousness to something that inspires you, 'excitement' perhaps? In this way you will gain a totally different perspective on life.
10. Notice your posture—replicate postures when you have been successful.

So how do we create positive dominant thoughts in our minds and cut out negative ones? Catch them! Start to become aware of when you are communicating negatively-when is it that you are most negative?

These are the tried and tested techniques used for low self-esteem sufferers who benefit greatly from cognitive behavioural therapy, which uses a similar philosophy in 'self talk' manipulation that we discussed earlier in this chapter.

What do you say to yourself? Do you go through in your mind before a contest or training session the outcome of the up and coming event? Do you consider winning and losing scenarios? It's always good to become aware of the possibility of losing, or developing skills in emotionally disassociating from past failures in a contests. However your dominant thoughts for the future should always be of winning. Dominant thoughts, if accepted by the unconscious transpire into reality.

When you are training are your dominant thoughts on how painful your sessions are? Is your focus on the fear that perhaps you will never achieve the desired level to accomplish your goals? Are you worried about whether you lose and what the consequences are for this? These examples can only hinder your performance. The more you think in this manner the more you confirm them. If you fear losing, your dominant thoughts are of losing. What you will need to do is to reassess them. In many cases you will find that there are specific phrases that you use consistently. Try to catch the phrase and change it to a positive one-you will find after sometime the positive phrase will become your default phrase. If for example you focus on the pain in a training session a better idea might be to decide what your motivation is that brings you to the gym. If it's the next up-and-coming event or to bench-press 300 pounds. Then focus on that goal and create a new phrase. Change the phrase 'my muscles are aching' (which focuses on aching) to 'My mind is in control' or 'My endurance is increasing with every repetition'.

Geoff, Bodybuilding mental blocks—case study 2.

Geoff was a Bodybuilder who came to me for advice on why he was able to build nearly every muscle group in his body, but large pectorals (chest) muscles still continued to elude him. There can be many obstacles to growth in bodybuilding and natural ability is only a part of it. Some people are just born with genetic advantages, advantages in upbringing, and social conditioning. Some athletes have a higher amount of muscle fibres in certain muscle groups compared to others, making it easier to build that group of muscle. However this is no reason why an individual cannot build their muscles to the maximum that their body will allow. I do not believe in the notion that one is stuck with genetic advantage / disadvantages, there are too many examples of amazing people who have overcome such setbacks and broken through these boundaries.

I believe we can amount to almost anything that we desire. Some have to work harder for results than others, but this only makes it more rewarding when success is achieved. All humans are capable of the same actions, as long as they create the mindsets that they need to accomplish that goal.

Geoff's problem I discovered went back all his bodybuilding life. He was a late developer as a teenager and always regarded himself as smaller in physical size than his peers. Even though he grew far larger than his peers in his later teens and went onto become a not insignificant bodybuilder this self-image stuck in the back of his mind. His chest was developed, but not in comparison to his other muscle groups. In bodybuilding symmetry this is exceedingly important to the athlete and when one muscle group lags behind it can result in much anxiety.

Geoff and I went about correcting this mental block of his. We worked on the notion that now he had grown-up and become an adult, it meant that he was now capable of increasing his chest muscles to coincide with his self-image. In this programme we set about a routine of self-hypnosis so that Geoff could continue to increase the effects of the hypnotic sessions I performed with those of his own. One aspect of the hypnotic script that he used was to feel the muscles in his chest become warm with the increased blood flow into the muscle. He was also instructed to imagine the muscle growing as he concentrated upon its warm sensation and the flow of growth hormone that would be drawn to the area. This had a two-fold effect. It directs the mind that it does indeed grow easily (remember the subconscious has no reasoning facility). Also blood is drawn to the area and pumps the muscle up, this increases the likelihood of muscle building and encourages the athlete, increasing his belief in the effects of self-hypnosis.

As we have seen, just directing the mind to have an effect upon the body can and does have a biological effect, cells reproduce, muscles build, injuries heal faster and fat is easily burnt.

Geoff was a bodybuilder, so as with many he had to push himself past the Machismo barriers which stated to him that he didn't need help. He was too tough to present himself to any type of sports therapist. Fortunately he overcame this perception and was subsequently able to make leaps ahead in personal development. His chest muscles began to grow with previously unseen proportions. The more his chest grew the more powerful his self-image and belief in the effects of hypnosis became. This increased the effects. There came a time when he no longer needed to concentrate on the chest and started to look at his body as a whole unit again. Geoff now has continued with his belief in hypnosis and especially self-hypnosis, this has enabled him to attain the body and personality that he requires. If there is something in his life that he does not want or anything he does want to gain, he has tools to move towards that goal.

With the continued use of hypnosis Geoff has been able to visualise his body the way he wants it to be, the shapes, feelings and even the strength that he desires are all attainable. And to think, all of these improvements just by setting aside a little time for himself each day!

Mental blocks are very powerful, both in sport and life generally. Our individual upbringings have a huge effect on our adult lives, these are the things that develop our personalities and the perceptions that we have of our lives experiences.

A lot of the time, as was partly the case with Geoff's chest development problem, our mental blocks are developed in childhood. We have difficulty in changing along side our self-images when we graduate into adult hood. Geoff had a perception that his chest muscles grew very slowly and this was a perception brought with him from his childhood days. Clearly children don't have large muscular physiques so his perceptions were perfectly rational for a child. If a person goes into adult hood at a later stage than his peers, internal communication can prevent the body from developing well in a particular way. We've seen that internal dialogue is powerful enough to change our body's in any which way we command it to, so this has to have an effect. It is self-perpetuating because the more we focus on the problem the stronger the command becomes. It was true that Geoff could not previously develop a chest. When he was a child, and when developing at puberty he was a late developer so this only reinforced his perception that he would never develop. This can in many cases create a fear of not developing, which in turn again strengthens the likelihood of the problem continuing. Together we were able to remove the old fear and develop new success strategies that were more in tune with Geoff's self image as an adult.

Chapter Four

Which Cheese is the Moon made of?
—*exploding the sports sponge.*

'Fire is the test of gold; adversity of strong men'
—Seneca

Cosmetic Weight Control—*energy in, energy out.*
Suggestion Hypnosis is one of the fastest and most effective ways I have found to assist in weight loss. We must be careful here to distinguish between the different types of hypnotic treatment for weight control. As a general rule it can be said that when a person has more than two stones to lose in weight (to reach their ideal body fat percentage) then suggestion Hypnosis may not be the treatment required. If there is more than two

stones to lose some form of 'root cause' treatment such as analytical hypnotherapy or psychotherapy might be the best answer. Another aspect that should be considered is whether the person in question has consciously tried losing weight, if they have had many attempts then it is clear they are incapable of losing the weight by themselves. There must be either an educational problem such as lack of dietary knowledge or incorrect exercise ability. Alternatively the cause might be unconscious; therefore some type of mind therapy is required from a professional who has knowledge of motivational causes.

If the client has merely put on a stone or so through lack of care and exercise, hypnosis is a superb and effective way to unconsciously shed those pounds. Interestingly enough from my experience of weight control hypnosis, the client does not even need to change their diet or exercise plan, I have had clients whose mind merely directs their metabolism to burn those excess calories and break up that immobile fat.

Weight Control is one of the simplest concepts in the world to grasp although with today's hectic lifestyles there are other aspects involved. If you create a calorie deficit you will lose weight, create a calorie surplus you will gain weight. You can not put on weight if you burn more calories than you eat, you can not lose weight if you consume more calories than you burn, *it seems so simple*, no complicated diets, or exercise plans in sight. This is simplified, but bear with me and we will discuss why the body may react by gaining weight when calories are reduced.

Essentially all food could be viewed as energy. Food is energy and the fat on our body is stored energy. If we have an excessive amount of stored energy (fat) on our bodies then it makes sense to reduce the amount of energy consumed (food) and to increase the amount of energy we burn (exercise).

One of the most effective diets for losing weight is a non fat diet. This is where the participant focuses on reducing the fat content in their diet. You have probably heard many a dieter claim that the only way to lose weight is reduce the fat in their diets, and it is not calorie counting but fat counting which is the most effective form of weight reduction. This is not true, fat reduction is indeed an effective form of weight control, but it's the reduction in calories brought on by a reduced level of fat which enables one to create a calorie deficit. Fat contains twice as much calorific content than either protein or carbohydrate, therefore a reduction in fat is extremely likely to reduce the amount of calories in ones diet, and it is this affect that creates results. So fat reduction diets are in reality calorie reduction diets, this is why they are effective, they cause a calorie deficit, and enhanced results are seen if calorie burning is practised simultaneously. Remember energy in—energy out.

Another reason for the enhanced results in reducing fat content is that fat when eaten is immediately absorbed as body fat and not used as energy straight away. Whereas protein or carbohydrates need the body's resources to convert them into body fat if a surplus of calories is present. This process in itself uses calories to convert the substance, therefore even more calories are used enhancing the likelihood that body fat will be reduced.

"But I love my food", a chorus of fatties will proclaim with a hint of sympathy in their voices. Those who say this are actually mistaken and it would be beneficial for them to realise this. Although they will protest and argue that in fact 'yes' they do love food, its one of their great pleasures in life, I will still maintain that they are in fact mistaken and it is the feelings and emotions that they *associate* with food that they enjoy.

Nothing in life in itself is enjoyable! That initially seems a confusing statement perhaps, although it's true. Realise that if an activity was enjoyable in itself then all human beings would partake in it, we would all enjoy the same things, because we all have the same neurology. In reality we don't all enjoy the same things, because throughout our lives we have developed very individual forms of personal evolution, we have all gained totally different perceptions and experiences of the world.

We have made neuro associations, which attach themselves to particular behaviours and actions. Almost always these associations are unconscious ones, intended in our primeval ancestral days to shield us from the dangers of life, and to develop our personal skills.

If you enjoy sport then the chances are that at some time in your life you had an experience that made you feel that you were good at that sport or you could imagine the rewards that being good at this sport would bring to you. It is often the case (especially in champions) that sports people can imagine the benefits bought on by the chosen activity. It might be the satisfaction that winning an event will bring them, or the financial gains from winning at their sport. It is not the sport itself that they enjoy, the pain of the long training sessions, pushing oneself to the limit is not enjoyable, in fact it can be quite the opposite. It is the associations linked to training that pushes the champion sports person. It could be the feeling of satisfaction of a personal best, or perhaps the recognition amongst their sporting peers and often it's a part of their self-image.

This type of drive is sometimes known as 'towards motivation', one is gaining motivation to push towards a goal. The opposite would be 'away from' motivation, an example might be the budding entrepreneur motivated away from the back street slums and poverty that he encountered as a child.

Now how does all of this fit in with Weight Control? Well, perfectly I would say, whether one is gaining or losing weight it is in my opinion vital to be aware of these mental links with ones behaviour. Being in control of your mind and body, and aware of the emotions that food has upon it will have a dramatic effects upon your diet plans. You will also gain the skill to put on or lose weight at will, or even stay at a constant weight without making an effort to plan food programs.

Motivation—*life's driving force.*

'People aren't lazy. They simply have impotent goals-that is, goals that do not inspire them'.

—Anthony Robbins, Unlimited power.

Many people believe they can generate motivation through setting inspiring goals. This is true for some but they often fail to realise the reasons behind the inspiring image, consequently it is more difficult to generate motivation on a constant basis, a skill we could all benefit from. Motivation is about knowing *why* you want a goal or activity, not *what* you want. Sure, knowing what you want is important because it gives you something to focus upon. The point is, if you want a particular goal, setting reasons why you want it is far more powerful than just visualising the outcome. It creates far more emotion to realise your underlying driving force. Suppose you wanted to build up a business to gain an income of a million pounds. Then the prospect of having a million pounds piled up in a thousand, one thousand pound bundles on the bedroom floor is not overly inspiring to motivate you to go out and achieve that ambition. You need to generate the reasons for wanting a million pounds or the outcomes of gaining that money. These might be; financial freedom; the house you would buy; the feeling of accomplishment in building a business; admiration from family and friends and any other positive trappings you'd like from that goal. It is this that generates the powerful effects of getting you up in the morning or pushing you through those times when things are not going so well. Sport is no different, clearly understanding the reasons why you want to excel creates a powerful motivator.

Another way of creating motivation is to set events or time frames that inspire you as targets. I have mentioned previously that time limits are futile in goal setting, the event time frames mentioned here are somewhat different. Although at the outset these two goal types seem similar, there are subtle but significant differences. In the case of 'event' organised goals you are trying to motivate yourself to reach set goals aimed at a specific event. The event once reached has no real significance. On the other hand if you set the goal towards a specific time or date in itself being a goal and the attainment of this goal was not achieved in that time frame, a level of frustration sometimes depression will be experienced. This is not a healthy way to exist.

Recently a client approached me regarding a sporting goal he wanted to motivate himself to achieve. After some time discussing his life and sporting ambitions I discovered that a couple of his friends were having a wedding anniversary. This seemed to be a good target to set some sporting goals for him to achieve. I made a wall chart and got specific weight and bodily conditions that he desired to attain within that time frame, and of course the reasons why he wanted to achieve them. This concept I find to be one of the best ways to motivate oneself. It encourages you to push yourself towards a goal, towards a specific condition. Together we conjured up enough associations of 'pain' in not achieving that goal so that he always felt like training at the times when there might be other tempting distractions that might disrupt his routine. When a distraction arose he consciously chose to think of painful consequences of not achieving his goal, this motivated him to act.

As soon as the anniversary had passed we discovered that for two weeks afterwards he hadn't been training on a constant basis as he'd done before, he'd begun slacking. I'm all for rest periods following long term stints of high level training, after all it's in the times of rest, not training, that the body builds muscle during recovery. Having justified this we still needed to realise that there might be more to this reduction in his motivation than a well earned recovery session. A new routine was planned, he finished the two weeks 'rest' and planned a goal to work towards that might inspire him. I needed perhaps to associate an inspiring reward for my client after some heavy training. He decided that it was time to book a holiday abroad for three months time, that was enough time to accomplish a good degree in his training sessions and was an opportunity to set another 'rest' period. The holiday destination was to be in a hot climate giving the additional inspiration of showing off his body on the beach. The more reasons one can develop to achieve a goal the more likely one is going to stick with the routine and accomplish it. More importantly you want reasons that are so compelling that you feel excited about training to reach them, this makes training fun. You'll no longer need to drag yourself up for a session, because you'll leap up in keen anticipation. You'll want to get in that gym.

Often sports and training is not just an activity, it's a part of your whole life and personality. Lets face it in today's western world people love to pigeon hole you and an athlete is one which they will readily acknowledge. The most mentally healthy view is to develop every area of your life from finances, relationships (romantic and general) hobbies, work, rest and of course sporting activities all in to one package. This means that one area should not over rule the others, you need to remain flexible in your approach. It's fine to have ambitions and to work hard towards a goal, but life is unpredictable and missing a training session is not the end of the world, after all we've already stated that rest is an important factor in the body's recovery and its build up.

Try not to let your training become an obsession, it's clear that when approaching an event or competition other areas of life need to take a back seat, but this is not the case throughout your entire life. By setting a wall chart in advance of training you will be able to chart and monitor when you train or miss a session. This way if you find yourself having to do other things you can rearrange the session without it affecting your actual training. It is sometimes easy to think you have been training quite heavily for a month, unfortunately when you check your records you realise that you have not trained consistently. The main reason I like monitoring my progress in this way is because I can look at my chart and see what and when I have trained. This enables me to take days off if I feel the need and to reschedule the routine so that I still train as often but in a different pattern. It means that I don't actually lose out on any training. This leads to a much healthier, more relaxed lifestyle.

Inspiring motivation is a fantastic bedfellow to weight control, especially in the sporting arena. The majority of sports people find the motivation of sports excellence great enough to break any patterns of weakness in their diet programmes, thus their bodily functions are being manipulated by their thoughts, visions, and images, in other words their minds. It still amazes me at how difficult people say it is for them to lose weight, the fact that they are born that way, they have poor genetics, they have special slow metabolisms etc… In reality they can lose weight, no matter how hard they convince themselves that it is impossible and the odds are stacked against them, no-one is saying it will be easy but it is possible. You probably know someone who makes such excuses, sometimes they seem plausible, however in most cases it is mis-leading nutritional information or lack of motivation that is the problem.

Watch this person as they are delivered a scenario in which they find an immense amount of motivation in themselves to get up and do something a little more pro-active about the situation.

One scenario that frequently pushes a 'fatty' into a position of action is the Wedding day of a Bride to be. The bride becomes motivated to go on a healthy eating diet and to perform some exercise in the months running up to their wedding. It's amazing how quickly they can see results when (as we know) they were genetically ungifted in the low body fat stakes only weeks beforehand.

We've already stated that Weight Control in theory is a simple goal to achieve, energy in—energy out. Create a calorie/energy deficit and you will lose weight. Create a calorie surplus and you will gain weight. Keep an equilibrium and one will stay at a constant desired weight. That's the physical side looked at. We've seen that this is true, but this book is all about *Sports Mind Power* and that's why I've included weight control in this book. I believe every area in ones life is created by ones own mind, all situations are results of our own desires, thoughts, actions and our perceptions of them. I have also stated that weight control is predicted by how many calories we consume related to how many calories we burn. Having said that one still has to battle against the mental aspects of weight control. In essence weight control, whether that means gaining or losing weight is about behavioural modification.

The Mind is the most powerful and influential aspect of our world, *'there is nothing with out first the mind'*. This is especially true in weight control, I get phenomenal results from weight control hypnosis. I believe weight control is almost entirely based in the mind, second only to our energy in—energy out behaviour patterns (although these are also controlled by our minds).

You may be thinking now that this all seems a bit like a vicious circle, and you'd be right. It is indeed quite difficult for some individuals to create action from their knowledge. In other words having the will power to resist that high calorific chocolate bar.

This is the most exciting part of weight control, the challenge of reworking our associations with food to create our own happiness. Would it not be a fantastic achievement if one could change ones association at will. For instance wouldn't it be most exciting to have the power to change the pleasure you receive from consuming your favourite chocolate bar (for instance) to consuming a healthier stick of celery? Even if at present you hate celery; the celery would give you the same feeling as the chocolate once did.

It might sound a little horrendous to give up one of your pleasures but remember you would not be giving up the pleasure in its self, the pleasure is still there you still receive that pleasure but from something quite different. You still get just as much pleasure from the celery as you once received from the chocolate. *'It can't be done'* I hear you exclaim. But it can. And it's the best way that I have come across to change any area of your life, which enables you to accomplish a goal without the tiresome battle against your will power.

In my work as a Hypnotherapist I come across a large number of people who would like to give up smoking. Clearly this is something they have failed to do in the past using will power, obvious by the fact that they were now approaching myself for hypnotherapy. One concept known among mind practitioners is the notion of 'symptom substitution'. Symptom substitution is a self-explanatory term used to describe a situation, which on occasion arises after therapy.

It was noted first by Sigmond Freud who discovered that sometimes when removing a problem or symptom from a patient that the person returned at a later date to reveal to his dismay that they had yet another problem. In these cases the subject would usually be overjoyed at the fact that the original problem of which they started therapy had vanished even though this new seemingly unrelated problem arose soon afterwards.

The reason for this seems to be that all symptoms have an underlying cause probably at an unconscious level. Now if one removes a symptom through Hypnosis or any other therapy, then the originating cause will still remain. It has not been removed. This cause will simply create another symptom in place of the other, therefore still communicating the problem to the patient at a conscious level—the whole essence of Hypno-analysis.

A cure for this conflict of the mind has been found in recent years. One which is not a wholly satisfactory solution for all problems but does suit many less deep-rooted problems such as smoking and sometimes overeating. Hypnotherapists have found that if one replaces the negative unwanted behaviour such as smoking with a more positive symptom then this will prevent the development of an unsatisfactory symptom created by the unconscious mind. One example might be gaining the symptom of 'having a great deal of pride and pleasure in giving up smoking', this can be seen almost entirely as beneficial to patients. There is little harm in replacing the perceived stress release created by smoking by a feeling of pride and pleasure! My point here is the realisation that one can direct ones mind in these areas to gain beneficial outcomes by simply noticing and acting upon causes and driving forces of ones behaviour. Once this is achieved one can move on to each area of your life and start to remould the way you perceive events both internally and externally.

Losing Weight—*weightlessly.*

'Our bodies are our gardens...our wills are gardeners.'
—William Shakespeare.

Eat breakfast to lose or to gain weight, that sounds like a contradiction but it's not. There is solid scientific reasoning behind this practice. Eating breakfast kick-starts the metabolic system early on in the morning. If you fail to eat breakfast then the metabolic system does not really get going until mid afternoon or whenever you have your first meal. The first meal of the day starts the energy burning process therefore you will benefit far more from starting the process early in the morning rather than at lunch time. If you don't get time for breakfast, grab a banana, there is nothing better in the morning, low in fat, high in water and carbohydrates.

What this says is that whether you are trying to lose weight or gain weight you need to get the body's system started after a night of fasting. If you try it and take breakfast at eight in the morning you will notice that you'll feel hungry at around ten O'clock. Usually this would not be the case until about twelve perhaps. The fact that you'll begin to feel hungry earlier is not necessarily a problem, you don't need to react to hunger, just acknowledge it and carry on. Hunger pangs are not a form of pain, people react too quickly to them at times. It's a signal that your stomach is empty and your metabolism has kicked in. Having said this if you are eating small quantities constantly throughout the day then you are far less likely to feel hungry. If you want to gain weight then make sure you eat at these times and perhaps in between, the golden rule for weight gain is six small meals a day.

Dieting—*the balancing act.*

'Nothing great was ever achieved without enthusiasm'

—Emerson

Getting fat on starvation diets!—If you stop eating your body will go into an 'emergency mode'; this is a throw back to our earliest ancestral days. The body will lose weight but the weight loss is Glycogen and water not fat (Glycogen is the most readily available source of energy in starvation circumstances). Low glycogen levels result in a slowing of the metabolic rate, so you gain weight more easily, because you burn fewer calories.

If one is unfortunate enough to experience a starvation situation, the human body is designed to store excess pounds of food consumed as fat. Therefore, if your body spends a certain amount of time with no food intake (crash dieting), it will increase the rate at which it stores fat once food consumption begins again. You will gain more body fat than before the diet! Interestingly selected nutritional deficiency also increases the appetite, so an unbalanced diet may result in an increase in hunger.

Calorie reduction is not enough to reduce body fat as during dieting muscle loss is the primary result. Increased levels of exercise will help retain muscle and increase fat reduction.

Eating smaller meals more often throughout the day helps to stabalise blood sugar and insulin levels. High levels of insulin will reduce fat burning abilities.

Enjoying your food more!—The brain takes around half an hour to receive the message that you are full regardless of the amount you have consumed in that time. This is why eating water rich foods such as melon slowly, is an ideal way to start a meal. Low in calories and rich in water content you are nearer to the 30-minute full signal once the main meal has been started. Conversely if you wish to gain weight, eating quickly will enable you to consume a larger quantity of food before your brain gives the body the 'full' message, resulting in gained body fat.

Reacting to hunger.—When you become focused on not eating you become obsessed with food and it becomes more difficult to stick to a diet, whatever you focus the mind on becomes your reality, trying not to eat is still focusing on food.

In western society we are programmed to believe that the things that are most precious are those substances which are least accessible or are lacking in great quantity. If you avoid the foods you really want or enjoy you will resent the whole process and the food will be on your mind. We want the process of dieting to be enjoyable, a level of happiness is required, sacrifices are not always the best policy even though they are just a matter of individual perception.

If you claim to enjoy food then it makes perfect sense to eat more slowly, thus enjoying the taste for longer. The faster you eat the less taste you will experience. This will mean a much more enjoyable existence, and the stomach will not become over loaded.

I have already mentioned in this section that a lot of people don't realise, and this goes throughout the whole spectrum of body types, you *do not have to react to hunger*! This belief astounds many, but it is true. If you keep your fat percentage and water levels at a healthy level there is no problem.

Vanilla crave control—Research presented to the 13th International Congress of Dietetics in Scotland suggests the mere smell of Vanilla can suppress food cravings. The findings of the 'Crave control patch' an appetite suppressant invented by Liz Paul, had surprising results of an average four pounds in weight loss over a one month period. The scented patches are sniffed whenever the dieter has a food craving and the craving is said to subside.

Using a small bottle of Vanilla food flavouring can have similar effects.

Stress—When we become stressed our bodies release hormones which slow down the metabolism and this has an effect of storing extra body fat. One reason for this process is that human evolution has concluded that during winter months a lack of food is likely and considered to be the main source of stress in our lives. Stress releases hormones and our bodies begin to store fat to out last the expected fasting, the problem lies in the fact that to modern man winter no longer means a shortage of food. However, our bodies continue to react by slowing down our metabolisms. The opposite effect is the release of Endorphins in the summer months when food supply is expected to be plenty and stresses reduced. Most evident today when people are far more happy and energetic during the sunnier seasons.

Hunger Signals—*mind / emotion strategies.*

'Human feelings are words expressed in human flesh'
—Aristotle.

The hunger process developed in our ancestral days. Designed to signal when the body was in need of food thus hunting/gathering required.

The obese, paranoid, self-protective person will jump to their own defence and exclaim 'but its painful to be hungry, I get pains in my stomach'. When you stop eating for a short while your stomach will become empty, this is the normal hunger process. The body's process was aware that the search for food often took some time thus the hunger pangs felt are initiated long before any health problems or starvation is near by. These pangs are clearly not danger signals, we can painlessly ignore hunger pangs for many hours with relatively no discomfort—remember you are in conscious control.

When dieting to lose weight hunger pangs can be seen as enjoyable signals that one is in control and a meal is required in the somewhat near future. It is great to acknowledge that your body is able to signal these processes unconsciously, it's really an amazing ability. If hunger pangs really do irritate you, a simple short term solution in avoiding high calorie snacking is to drink some water, it's low in calories, it will fill the stomach enough to stop the pangs, you'll gain energy from the water and you won't ruin your natural diet. Having said this hunger pangs should be relatively absent if you are eating regularly in the correct proportions. The distinction between pangs and cravings is an important one.

Cravings are slightly different from hunger because for cravings hunger does not need to be present. They are more about how we represent things and their associations than with the food itself. Animals don't crave certain foods for any other reason than if they need the nutrition with in that food. This can be seen in pregnant women also. The body needs a vitamin, mineral or substance of some sort and the mind sets about causing this person to crave a food with intense desire. All this is activated at an unconscious level, often with astounding results. It is seen to be the case that in many instances a pregnant woman's mind combines unbelievable strange mixtures of food which in previous circumstances the female would have rejected in disgust. The psyche is able to manipulate the mind to actually enjoy this combination and even enjoy foods that previously the person hated the taste of.

This is a good example of how our bodies are able to encourage us to crave foods unconsciously and sometimes this can work against us, for example to remain over weight for the feeling of protection it brings.

Bulking up—*infinite dimensions.*

'There is no success with out hardship'

—Sophocles.

To gain 1lb of body weight per week you need to consume 500—1000 calories in addition to your normal calorific intake that keeps your body weight stabilised.

Eat six small meals per day—this is the magic number for ultimate weight gain. They don't need and should not be huge meals, but smaller ones that save energy reserves and fuel our muscles effectively.

Try modelling a fat persons eating habits if you wish to put a little fat content onto your body frame, after all they are the experts in weight gain! Perhaps you might like to change some of the things they consume, but in general copy their eating patterns, the speed that they eat and attitude towards food. Be careful not to fall into eating their 'type' of diet for long periods. It's often high in fat and bad for the heart.

Muscle takes 22% less space than fat, so having a high level of muscle you can weigh far heavier whilst still remain smaller and more shapely. This is one explanation why many women become disheartened with training. They begin weight training and muscle starts to become more toned and shapely, this has an effect of increasing surface areas such as their thigh muscles. Fat tends to take a little while to start to reduce so this combination of high calorie burning muscle growth and slow fat burning makes the female trainer feel her legs are getting fatter by training! Clearly she will soon give up her training in dismay. The truth is that if she continued she would have passed this equilibrium and her legs will look far slimmer. In addition more muscular thighs has an effect of burning fat more quickly, thus reducing the likelihood of putting weight back on again.

Another weight control phenomena is the body's quest to remain at a constant weight, said to last up to four years. Consequently if you attempt to lose or gain weight the body tries to bring it's self back to the former weight level. The metabolism will adjust it's self accordingly. The solution again is weight training or more specifically muscle enhancement.

(See the introduction to the 'weight gain for bodybuilding' script for more information on bulking up.)

Alison, Weight Loss—case study 3. *Half a stone per week no diet changes.*

Alison came to see me for weight loss Hypnotherapy. She was in her mid twenties, had a good career and secure relationships. Her life seemed relatively stress free and she was happy with it except for the problem she felt that she had; too much fat content.

Personally I don't believe in weighing people to discover their weight, it is not particularly accurate or important. It's a persons body fat percentage that determines whether one is healthy or not. It's a high fat percentage that is responsible for problems such as heart attacks and high blood pressure not the weight of a person. Weighing someone on scales is a way of weighing their whole body, bones included. These are all variable. 'Body fat percentage' not only monitors fat but also muscle, bone and water content too, an important factor in women as they often hold water during menstrual cycles.

A vast amount of bodybuilders are over weight when related to the charts that are devised to monitor weight. In reality they have low body fat and high muscle percentages, this puts their weight up to obese standards which is mis-leading. In simple terms you cannot get away from the fact that if one looks in the mirror whilst naked, it is relatively easy to notice the saggy bits that are fat, thus determining weight control needs. This said one must be aware of people's mis-conceptions about their own bodies and the rising awareness of eating disorders clarifies the problems. There are vast differences in people's perceptions of their own bodies and how they should be. If in doubt seek professional help.

Once body fat is established one can then use scales to monitor how much they need to lose now that they are aware of the amount in pounds of body weight which is fat.

Alison was the type of client who was unhappy with her figure, but certainly not in the bracket of someone who has unconscious causes that may hinder our therapy. It was a good signal that she had a secure life with a supportive partner. People's lives often tell you much more than some realise. This is often confirmed after therapy, when every area of the persons life just seems to drop into place.

I explained to Alison the types of therapy and what I could do for her, she was happy and quite insistent to commencing suggestion therapy. I saw her for one hour a week for several weeks. This is not always the case, usually one or two sessions is good enough, but I wanted some feed back from Alison and she was happy to do so. In addition she wanted the commitment from me. Several booked sessions meant to her that I would have a duty to continue if the therapy did not work (people are very pessimistic about hypnosis-initially).

After the first session Alison lost half a stone,* which she was very pleased about. She came bounding into my office full of optimism ready for her next session. I questioned Alison about her diet in the last week and she was a little ashamed that she had changed nothing. She still ate her favourite chocolate bars and did no exercise at all. Although it's good to have the dietary assistance when practising weight loss hypnosis, I was secretly quite pleased about this occurrence. It is not always easy to monitor the effectiveness of hypnosis in areas such as weight loss because patients have this habit of trying a lot harder when they are assisted by a therapist., therefore helping the perceived effects of the hypnotherapy. Another issue is that when one is paying for any sort of therapy people tend to have a commitment to success. They don't like the idea of wasting money, and the higher the fee the stronger the will to succeed. This makes it difficult to attribute the hypnosis to the weight loss solely. Alison was one of the cases where she was not interested in 'trying', she was going to let hypnosis do all the work.

I was glad to see that Alison continued to lose the weight week after week, at smaller but significant amounts and it turned out that she has kept the weight off ever since. And certainly she was happy with the results.

I and many others have found that hypnosis is very effective in the assistance of weight loss, with other variables consistent it can reduce body fat by itself. Interestingly the reason seems to be all down to the mind and the imagination. Cosmetic weight loss is far more effective when imaginations of visual images are added. These as I've mentioned before, do not need to be real in a physiological sense, one can use ones own imagination to dream up images of the fat distributed in all manners of ways. There could be little men in the body digging with shovels in the layers of fat and distributing it around the body in wheel barrows, if that is how the client feels most comfortable in doing so. The unconscious mind has no reasoning it just needs a direction and a goal to be delivered with clarity and persistence to achieve it. Thoughts, feelings and strong emotions can only assist in this process.

Half a stone per week can be seen as an unhealthy amount to lose. As a general rule two pounds per week is the maximum amount one should safely reduce by. One reason for this is that losing more than two pounds per week of fat is unlikely, the weight loss then becomes water or muscle loss which is undesirable. It is best to consult an expert in this area if one decides that more than two pounds per week is desirable. You can then be monitored regards to fat, muscle and water levels in the body.

Summary;

You can eat the fattening foods that you enjoy and lose weight, as long as you burn more energy than you consume.

Ways to create an energy deficit;

- Increase exercise-this can be anything from walking, dancing, swimming or any conventional sport.
- Reduce the amount of calories consumed -this may be achieved by reducing fattening foods or reducing the overall Calories consumed.
- The easiest and most effective way to lose weight is to combine - increasing Calories burnt (exercise) and decreasing Calories consumed.
- You don't have to react to hunger!
- The easiest way to reduce Calories is to reduce fat intake as it contains much more Calories per gram than protein or carbohydrate. That way you might not need to reduce the amount you consume and there is less risk of adding extra fat.
- The Chinese eat 20 % more food than Westerners but are 25% thinner! Due to the quality of food they eat—*less fat.*
- Sniff Vanilla flavouring when food cravings are experienced.
- Using visualisation (hypnosis) can produce remarkable improvements in your body condition, and mobilise fat deposits. Any form of relaxation helps with weight control due to the stress reduction experienced.

- Drink water if you are hungry when it's not a scheduled mealtime.
- Purchase a Pedometer to monitor your daily activity. Just by increasing the amount of activity you do to between 8000 and 10000 steps per day will significantly reduce your levels of body fat.

Part Two

Chapter Five

▼

Hypnosis
—humankind's dreamweaver.

'Silence is the Warriors art—and meditation is his sword'
—Dan Millman, 'way of the peaceful warrior'.

Structures of Magic—*the countless perceptions of hypnosis.*

Hypnosis and Hypnotherapy are shrouded in misconceptions and fallacies of a massive nature. Many perfectly intelligent and well educated people retain the most ridiculous opinions about hypnosis. It wasn't so long ago that a friend of mine volunteered to be a subject in a stage hypnosis act for entertainment purposes. After some time and several inductions by the hypnotist, the performer retained a selection of the volunteers and sent the rest away. This is common practice in stage performance, the so-called "hypnotisable" subjects are kept for use in the show, the "unhypnotisable" ones sent away. This is where one misconception arises, no one is unhypnotisable. Certainly I have yet to meet such a person. My friend who was one of these volunteers sent off stage claimed to me that she could not go into hypnosis. If you or I could not go into hypnosis, then we could not do virtually any of our everyday activities. As I will explain later the definition of hypnosis is vague and difficult to state, partly due to diverse range of personality types but mainly due to the varying levels of consciousness.

Every person in this world goes into hypnosis at least twice a day, when you go to sleep at night and when you awaken in the morning. You have to go through this level some call hypnosis, to get from being awake and conscious to being asleep and unconscious, that is hypnosis. Other times in our lives when hypnosis naturally occurs is during daydreaming which is a type of visualisation. In this case, one is becoming more focused on a given subject and less aware of their outer experiences, although in hypnosis one is more aware at an unconscious level. This brings with it increased awareness of the body's senses.

If you did not have the ability to go into hypnosis you would not be able to do many other everyday tasks. Such a task would be mathematics, you would not be able to visualise in your mind sums or calculate them to any degree. Watching television would be a problem as it would be difficult to become associated with characters and plots, without imagining yourself in those rolls. We will discover later how this type of association is very powerful in 'sporting behaviour change'. Modern research has found that hypnotisability is directly related to intelligence and concentration.

I think these examples show that every human being is capable of hypnosis to varying levels, so how is it that the hypnotist was unable to hypnotist my friend? Well, there may be a number of reasons for this. One is that the level of competence of the individual hypnotist is a varying factor one should take into account. If a hypnotist has little ability to change his repertoire to suit individual personalities then he will out of necessity come across some participants who have little rapport with him. The professional hypnotist should have the ability to adapt his routine to suit everyone. If the subject finds it hard to go into hypnosis then he must change to find an induction that suits the person in question. This brings with it obvious problems when hypnotising groups of people on stage. The hypnotist must use a reasonably quick routine that will hypnotise as many of his participants as possible so the show can continue.

Another factor with stage hypnosis is that each participant must be willing to go into a hypnotic state at a conscious level. If they fear what might occur on stage this may result in some anxiety and cause resistance to comply with the suggestions. Having said that it could be reversed and the resistance used to actually hypnotise the resistant person in question. However, this would invariably need the individual attention of the hypnotist, which is not usually available on stage.

With all of these factors put together you can see that people witnessing hypnosis can have their own conclusions and different perceptions of what is happening. It seems that hypnotics on stage are doing unconscious things against their will, in fact just by agreeing to go on stage the person is unconsciously agreeing to comply with the suggestions. If the hypnotist ever suggests something that is fundamentally against an individuals moral standard then he or she will rapidly become consciously aware again and flip out of hypnosis. The only thing that people who know nothing about hypnosis see, is the apparent control of a hypnotist over the subject, and this increases the perception that hypnosis is a weird and magical concept. In reality anyone with a small amount of knowledge can create hypnosis deliberately, indeed everybody already does it unconsciously many times everyday.

I find many people have misconceptions due to being unaware as to when a stage hypnotic is in or out of 'trance' and therefore a lot of confusion develops about how hypnosis works.

In therapy, hypnosis is used to bypass the critical consciousness to gain access to the powerful unconscious mind. It is then that either Psychotherapy is undertaken to release undesirable unconscious neurotic behaviour or suggestions are used to alter thoughts, feelings and behaviours. In suggestion therapy Post Hypnotic suggestions are used, they act after the therapy is discontinued, usually in the form of positive affirmations to assist in self-esteem, performance enhancement etc.

The Stage performer will use these 'Post Hypnotic Suggestions' often in the form of what we call 'triggers'. Triggers are types of neuro links in the mind, usually temporary suggestions delivered whilst in a hypnotic state. For example the stage performer may suggest that the hypnotic will jump up from the chair in which he is sitting on cue when a pre-arranged song is played, he might dance around the stage thinking he is Elvis. The link between the piece of music, the act and behaviour of thinking one is Elvis is the 'Trigger'. This trigger acts after the person is 'awoken' from trance and thus can be known as a 'Post Hypnotic Suggestion'.

To the audience all of this seems very magical, it appears that the hypnotist has some sort of power over the hypnotic. The audience fail to see all the work that has previously been conducted by the hypnotist of hypnotising and delivering the suggestions. Remember hypnosis is a state of altered awareness, it is not sleep, or even unconsciousness, but the consciousness is more focused and can be said to be altered from normal waking states. The effects of suggestions are greatly increased in these states, what psychologists' term 'hyper-suggestibility'. Incidentally hyper-suggestability can be heightened in other ways other than hypnosis. Fear has a similar effect upon the psyche.

The hypnotic often has no recollection of these post hypnotic suggestions (although one can access any given suggestion if one is persistent enough) and will make all sorts of excuses for their behaviour. Again to the audience of a performance much of the underlying techniques are oblivious to them. A hypnotist will often use a trigger to access the level of trance when he wants a subject to drop back into hypnosis at a given time. The hypnotist will suggest in trance something along the lines of 'When I say the words '*Sleep*' you will drop back into this level of relaxation immediately'. After this suggestion is delivered at any point during the show when the hypnotist wants the hypnotic to stop what he is doing, the hypnotist will say the word '*Sleep*' and he will drop back into trance. Usually there is also a behaviour associated with the word such as the clicking of fingers in front of the subject's eyes. The audience is still unaware of these techniques and will be impressed by the magic of hypnosis.

Post hypnotic suggestions are very powerful techniques in the use of therapy. Every suggestion that enters the consciousness, if accepted by the unconscious part of the mind, is automatically transformed into reality. This is what the Clinical Hypnotherapist aims to achieve, to alter unconscious behaviour by bypassing the critical conscious part of the mind.

Hypnosis is a powerful tool for change, especially in the alteration of behavioural addictions. A key point often overlooked is that we are all responsible for our own change, whether that is achieved with the help of an expert or otherwise. A fellow hypnotherapist once told me about a smoker who approached him for a session or two of smoking cessation hypnosis. The smoker was hypnotised and in the usual manner everything went very well. Upon completion of the therapy the patient diligently walked out of the consulting room and into the street outside, where he proceeded to withdraw a cigarette packet from his pocket and begin to light up and smoke the cigarette. This was a conscious decision on the client's side; he had every intention before the session to go through the therapy and return outside to 'test' its effectiveness. Clearly the hypnotherapist was quite perplexed about the attitude of the client and proceeded to explain to the smoker the full nature of hypnosis.

There is a saying in the hypnosis industry that 'all hypnosis is self-hypnosis'. To change a behaviour pattern such as smoking one needs the assistance of both the unconscious and conscious minds. It is far more effective to go through a session of hypnosis and want the desired result at a conscious level. There is absolutely no point deciding that you are about to push the limits of your unconscious by trying to break the work of hypnosis. Hypnosis is a very powerful tool for unconscious change when used intelligently, and certainly far more powerful than using the conscious mind alone.

Hypnosis is not a control mechanism, you can at times override the unconscious mind. This can be seen when smokers decide to use their will power to stop smoking, the unconscious behaviour is still there although it is suppressed by conscious reasoning. There are instances when hypnosis can override conscious decisions. One can install unconscious thoughts and feelings that are out of reach of the consciousness even when one knows they are irrational actions. For instance if I chose to hypnotise a client for smoking cessation by using a form of aversion therapy, I might decide to suggest that every cigarette smoked will taste of black rubber. Now this suggestion would be quite effective due to the nature of smoking, tar in cigarettes is very similar to burning rubber; thus this suggestion would quite easily take effect. The smoker would know that this has been suggested and also realise that the cigarettes they are used to smoking have not changed in taste, but their own perceptions have done. No conscious reasoning could alter this. The cigarette will still taste of burning rubber, but the smoking behaviour would have ceased by the time the 'rubber taste effect' had worn off.

The main point in all of this is to always remain in charge of your responsibilities, and don't go about trying to shift blame for your inability to change by yourself. It is always a good idea to inlist the help of a professional if your have failed to accomplish a goal at some stage in life. Professionals usually have more experience and more knowledge about your problem than you will have. Therapists are there to assist in change, they have many strategies to help you to gain the results that you need, but ultimately the buck stops with you. It's all too easy to blame a Psychotherapist or Hypnotherapist for not doing his job well enough when you fail to achieve what you had hoped. Hypnosis is an area where this perception is exaggerated, people often expect a magic solution. Hypnosis is a powerful tool for change and can help in an infinite number of ways, but the therapist also needs feedback from the client so he can be as flexible as possible. If you are not getting the desired result from your therapy, then communicate this to the therapist so that he can explain what is happening (because often people are unaware of changes happening when they do occur). Alternatively he can use some other tools in his repertoire to assist you even more.

Analytical Hypnotherapy—*the precept of cause and effect.*

'Show me a sane man and I will cure him.'
—C.G.Jung. Observer, 19 July 1975.

In any type of hypnosis the hypnotic subject need not believe in the power or ability of Hypnosis. Hypnosis acts on the unconscious part of the brain therefore needs no conscious acceptance.

Analytic Hypnotherapy is psychotherapy aided by hypnosis. It is now beginning to be widely recognised as a superior form of psychotherapy in its ability to 'draw out' underlying causes of neurotic thoughts and behaviours. Many forms of Hypno-analysis use what is known as 'free association', a system developed by Sigmund Freud. Free association is the freedom for the analysand to give over their thoughts and feelings during therapy. Over several weeks this is said to give clues to unconscious behaviour by revealing the unconscious cause, this in turn releases the neurosis forever. During therapy some form of abreaction is expected which brings about a cathartic effect. The symptom for which therapy was sought will now cease due to the 'release' of the 'repressed' underlying 'cause'. It needs to be noted that only around fifty percent of the benefits of analysis takes place in the therapists consulting room, the rest occurs in between sessions. Just one reason for the sessions being set at weekly intervals.

Analytical hypnotherapy is distinct from 'suggestion therapy' in that analytical therapy uses the condition of hyper-suggestibility to a lesser degree. The analytical hypnotherapist will induce the state of hypnosis using a similar technique of relaxation, however analytical therapy goes on to cut out verbal and non-verbal suggestions. The analysand is then encouraged to convey their thoughts and feelings as they appear in their minds rather than absorbing the therapists suggestion.

Analytical therapy is seldom seen for the treatment of sports therapy, but it does emphasis the notion of how an idea that has taken root in the subconscious always transpires into physical reality. More surprising is that the human is seldom aware of the motivation behind the behaviour due to its subconscious nature, sometimes blissfully unaware of the symptom itself at an intellectual level.

Dangers of Hypnosis—*taking control of your life.*

Life's too short to be afraid

—Robbie Williams.

No harm can be done through the use of auto or hetero hypnosis, it's a naturally occurring state. Even so there still remains the scepticism and suspicion about hypnosis and its use, even in this day and age, where medical doctors, psychiatrists and dentists frequently use the skill. You can attain Phd's in the discipline of hypnosis now that we are more aware of its benefits in so many areas of life. There is really nothing strange or magical about hypnosis and the wide spread use of hypnosis in sports is gradually coming to light. The state of 'hyper-suggestibility' witnessed in hypnosis is relatively indistinguishable from other forms of relaxation. Suggestion works in and out of hypnosis; ask any advertising agency!

Sports people are scared to admit their use of hypnosis mainly due to the possible reaction of less aware people who may brandish them as cheats. Everyone uses hypnosis on a daily basis, even though it is not necessarily done so consciously. The runner accesses his own internal world and blocks out the aching muscles and negative internal dialogue that endurance activities bring. This is called 'running high' in psychology. Essentially self hypnosis, no different from the hypnotist's old routine of swinging a watch on a chain in front of the patient, slowly reducing the speed with the rhythm of their breathing, gradually making their eyes feel drowsy.

Contrary to popular belief hypnosis has been used extensively in sport for at least fifty years. In his book 'Hypnosport' Les Cunningham comments that:

> 'In the 1956 Melbourne Olympic Games the Russian team supported a contingent of eleven hypnotists, a contingent with the charter to instil confidence and the will to win into the Russian athletes. Since the 1952 Helsinki Olympics, the Russians had been the leading medal winners in four out of seven Olympic games. In the other three games they ran a close second.'

So, its clear that we all, especially sports people use forms of hypnosis extensively and the use of a professional sports hypnotist can only enhance the benefits. A sports hypnotist will be able to assist the development of particular arousal levels in an athlete on cue to certain prearranged stimuli. It's certainly not desirable for an athlete to practise self-hypnosis developing an arousal level of complete relaxation then accessing that state when in the competition arena!

In previous chapters we have discussed many of the fears of hypnosis and accepted them as fallacies. However the main attribute to most fears is the perception one has of losing control. It is wrong to suggest that the Hypnotherapist is in control; 'all hypnosis is self hypnosis.' Using hypnosis or meditation is in fact a process of regaining inner control, the therapist is there to coach you in the skills needed. If you are living your life tense and anxious then the external environment is controlling your mind and body. By seeking relaxation you are taking back that control to enjoy life more fully. We can see this train of thought beginning to filter into the 'self-help' industry, therapists are now advising less emphasis on developing your own personality but more towards the improvement of one's environment. Consequently your personality will moderate to accommodate these changes, it's a form of organic growth rather than forced development. This philosophy goes back to the ancient ideas of Martial Arts;

water flows down hill, going with the flow not against it, however, slowly but surely water still has the ability to cut through rock!

A lack of knowledge sometimes encourages people to blame hypnosis for their own stupidity. Someone who leaves a hypnotherapy clinic and pays no attention to the road will readily blame the previous hypnotherapy session and it's effects when they subsequently get ran over by a bus. The client will in all probability convince themselves that they were still in trance, it's the fault of hypnosis. If the same scenario occurred following a dentist appointment (for example) the patient would not think twice about who is to blame. They will admit that they were not paying attention to the traffic. These excuses will carry on for days, if an accident occurs even weeks later people often blame hypnosis, they just somehow never really felt right after the session!

A related fear to the accident scenario is the fear of never waking up once a trance is achieved. This can not occur. Some people go deeper than others (somnambulistic) but we all fluctuate our levels of depth through out sessions of hypnosis. Those who go quite deep, are at times harder to bring back to full consciousness but the reason for this is in the subjects own mind. They enjoy the relaxing feeling of hypnosis, the feeling of having no cares in the world, for this reason they wish to remain in trance for a while longer. If the subject is left they will do one of two things; go into deep sleep or wake up half an hour or so later. Most professional hypnotherapists have techniques to bring difficult clients back to consciousness.

The Syntax of Hypnosis—*how to hypnotise using hetero and auto-hypnosis.*

'You can observe a lot just by watching'
—Yogi Berra, Baseball Manager.

The forms and definitions of hypnosis vary greatly. For the sports person relaxation inductions are the most beneficial. This is the type of hypnosis that will be performed at your local hypnotherapy centre if therapy is undergone. As we've seen the only real difference between sleep and hypnosis is that in hypnosis ones unconscious attention is amplified, in sleep the case is reversed.

In the following Chapters on Scripts and Induction's you will find out more about the stages of hypnosis and why they occur. In this section I will explain these stages and how elements in them interlink to varying degrees.

Stage One;

The first stage is the *Induction*. This is the part that is going to 'put' you into an altered state or level of awareness. The main point of this section is to cut out external stimuli creating relaxation so that one is able focus attention on to the given area or problem. These scripts will vary considerably and should be altered to the individual person both delivering and receiving the script. An experienced hypnotherapist will have the skills to induce an altered state in a matter of seconds and doesn't necessarily need to even mention the use of Hypnosis, however this is not what we are trying to achieve. We are seeking to develop a progressive level of body relaxation whilst keeping the mind sharp and focused on the desired task to be achieved.

Relaxation is one key to hypnosis and it is perhaps a good idea to notice how animals use relaxation, because animals do what they know works rather than the fads and fashions of what society tells them. Relaxation is based on sudden changes from tension to relaxation. In Hypnosis we use this in a comparative way. The more tense one feels, the greater the perceived amount of relaxation achieved when the tension is removed. The tension might also be in the form of vigorous activity, which also has the effect of muscle tension. This is the principle I was referring to when one observes a cat or dog preparing to relax or sleep. You will notice that the animal stretches before relaxing, this tenses the muscle and the aftermath is relaxation.

To achieve the desired result in hypnosis it might be best to lie down somewhere quiet and peaceful, somewhere you are unlikely to be disturbed. If you turn the phone off for a while that might help you to relax, as you'll be aware that no one will disturb you. Sitting in a comfortable chair is another choice and probably a better one. If you are tired after work or training perhaps, it is all to easy to drop to sleep when relaxing. Even though this is OK, in the view of hypnosis it is usually better to keep relatively alert in order to give yourself those positive suggestions. If you tape your suggestions or use someone else's then falling asleep might be less of a worry because the suggestions will still be running. This said sleep is not what we need to achieve here, so get comfortable, but not too much.

Now you need to try to relax as much as possible, remember this is your time set aside to relax, you really have nothing to do for the next hour because this is more beneficial and important to you than anything else.

Once you feel relaxed you'll need to follow the instructions given on the section in this book named Induction's. These are ways to deepen your relaxation even further than you are at this stage. The main way to achieve this is to relax and concentrate on each group of muscles of the body individually. Moving from one end of the body to the next. Going up the legs, torso, arms and neck all the way to the head. Make sure that your jaw is relaxed because this is an area that most often holds a great deal of tension. One way to release this is to move it a little and then to rest it at a slightly opened position as you relax. This is its natural position. Start to concentrate on your breathing, slowly, deeply but naturally.

As you have concentrated on relaxing your muscles this has had the effect of focusing your attention away from the outside world, the outside world has become disassociated thus less important for the time being. This is good because it's often the outside world that causes the tensions in ones body so this process has helped you to become even more relaxed. By now, even though you might not be aware of it, you have reached a level of relaxation and Hypnosis. Your face muscles will feel dense and your body will begin to feel either lighter in weight or heavier in weight on the surface beneath you, it could be lighter or heavier, people experience one or the other.

It's such a wonderful feeling; it amazes me why people don't use self-hypnosis far more often. The benefits are enormous and it feels so good to take an hour of each day to relax and visualise. Things become so much clearer in ones life. When you become more experienced in Hypnosis you will be able to drop into this state instantly, thus cutting down your time to half an hour each day for this relaxation, or even fifteen minutes.

Stage Two;

The Hypnotic Scripts are the details required for change, they are the lyrics to your improvement, they should be constructed in the positive. These scripts will be suggestions directed towards the 'problem' that you are focusing upon, it is now that one creates a clear picture upon the details that need to be altered, the thoughts, feelings, and sounds of the given scenario.

You'll see an explanation of such scripts in *Chapter Seven* in the section entitled *'Constructing Scripts for Sport and Life'*. Each script is specifically constructed for individual types of sport has an introduction explaining about hypnosis, plus the problems and benefits that you may encounter in the sport outlined. It would be of great benefit to you if you read all of these scripts and in particular their introductions, even if you have no interest in that individual sport. There are some useful points in all of them and additional statements that you might like to alter for your script. Scripts can become quite elaborate tales with metaphors and complicated analogies when constructed by professional hypnotherapists. There is no real reason why you need to over complicate to such a degree. For you the best and most effective option would be to keep it simple and to the point. Research suggests that this is the best method for the self-hypnotist.

Stage Three;

I have attached the third stage to the scripts in section two. This is where one imagines stepping into the finished product after therapy has ceased, seeing oneself accomplishing the goal. This is an optional part although it does prove to be both very effective and really quite fun! This is the part that I like the most. Who in their right mind would not like visualising the finished process, being the person who you have always wanted to be, act, look and feel like? It's a wonderful feeling!

The section involves imagining a scenario where you have acquired the skills you are looking for, the person you have become after you have achieved your goal. This sends a very strong signal to your nervous system of your abilities. Remember your subconscious (therefore your nervous system and body) has no logic, it does not reason. If you visualise your goals attainment with conviction, it will signal to the mind and body that this is true, and it will attain it for you. Even your motor responses are documented to react to thoughts such as these. This is an amazingly effective process for building muscles in particular areas or correcting performance problems and behaviour.

The introduction to 'Scripts' will explain how different forms of visualisation will help you to achieve your goal; it explains why visualisation works and the motivation behind it. It will also explain more about suggestion and its role in Hypnosis.

Finally, another stage perhaps is repetition. If you don't constantly use these processes your body cannot transmit them to reality. Today's heavy schedules mean it is often impossible to do this every day, but it's not impossible to have a total commitment to cutting out negative thoughts and emotions. We can all do this, and eventually it becomes natural and we can stop trying! There are also countless times in the day when there are sixty seconds spare to visualise the things that one dreams of in life. Waiting at a bus stop or in the queue for the cash point, take that time to send massive, powerful, visual images to the subconscious, mix them with feelings to break that barrier to the unconscious. Only then will it assist you in the attainment of your desires. Saturate your mind with positive images.

Signs of Hypnosis—*mother natures Bio-feedback guide.*

'All cases are unique, and very similar to others'.
— T.S.Eilot.

One of the main aspects of being an effective hypnotist is to be able to become sensitive to people's unconscious reactions. Hypnosis is about 'Bio-Feedback' as much as technique. Following are some signs that one can see in the hypnotic and some signs that the hypnotic may experience internally themselves, signs that are not accessible to the observer.

Observable.

1. Facial Flush during hypnosis due to increased blood flow.
2. Tingling sensation on the face. Associated side effects might also be 'pins and needles' in the hands and feet, ceasing moments after the hypnotic state is left.
3. Signs of sleep.
4. Increased level of awareness of all senses, temperature, smells, hearing and taste etc.
5. Emotional reactions such as crying, usually intellectually unexplainable-*not usually present in self-hypnosis but certainly present in assisted psychotherapy.*
6. Abnormal amounts of swallowing—dry mouth.
7. Cramp and muscular rigidity in hand and legs, subsides post hypnotically.
8. Respiration and heart rate will slow.
9. Slump of posture—relaxation, head falling forwards or to the side.

Unobservable.

1. Alpha brain wave activity will slow down.
2. Electrical resistance of skin will drop by around 20%—observable by way of a bio-rhythm counter.
3. Lightness and floating sensation throughout session.
4. Time distortion, roughly two times that of the session, an hour session will be distorted to a 20 minute session in the eyes of a hypnotic.
5. Reduction in blood pressure.
6. Release of Endorphins in the brain—the happy hormone causing a happy smiling hypnotic after the session is complete.
7. Increased imaginative abilities.
8. Pacifying effect on the Central Nervous System due to Pituitary Gland hormone releases.
9. Critical left brain activity is reduced allowing greater access to the creative right side of the brain.

Bridget, equestrian phobia/injury—Case study 4.

One aspect of sport psychology that makes it so interesting is the diversity of problem areas and the types of sport that are encountered.

Bridget approached me somewhat nervously, as is often expected in the field of hypnosis. She was unsure whether a hypnotist would be able to help her with her problem. It is always evident to me that if someone has plucked up the courage to eventually seek help, then their problem is beyond their own conscious abilities to solve, or else they would have done so. People often keep mind therapies as a last resort due to both the fear and stigma often associated with them.

Bridget was a cross country horse jumper (eventer). As with most 'horsey' people her interest went far beyond a hobby but spilled into every area of her life. The people around her were beginning to become concerned for her well being, she had started to become easily upset, anxious and short tempered. Bridget was well aware of her irrational behaviours and that they had only begun to emerge after an accident that she had experienced nearly a year before during a competition.

After some time it became clear that the accident although not physically a problem any longer, had many repercussions at a mental level. Her new fear which bordered on a phobic response, had seeped into her private life. The anxiety she experienced just from the fact that she was no longer able to enjoy her sport to the degree that she had previously, was enough to cause a huge amount of frustration. The resulting release of everyday worries that horse riding was able to promote was no longer an outlet for her pent up emotions. There was a void in her life.

We had to approach this problem in a multi-pronged attack. Firstly we had to discover her intial fear and decide why this was holding her back. With this removed some of the other areas of her life should slip back into place, if not other factors would be focused upon. In hypnosis it's often best to focus on one area at a time, although usually other factors are hard to distinguish from one than another.

Bridget realised that it was a past accident, a fall at a jump during competition that was the foundation of her fears. She had broken a leg after her horse had fallen on her. Although her physical injury had healed the mental ones were still clearly evident. It made her angry to doubt her abilities as a jumper, even at the most trivial of obstacles. She felt nervous and hesitated before jumps, consequently the horse would pick this up and lose confidence in the direction he should take. Bridget knew too well what she was capable of intellectually but found difficulty in harnessing her physical reactions to the external environment. It is interesting to note the physical aspects in humans that elevate animal reactions to our fears. When we are anxious we emit hormones called Pheromones. These are easily picked up by animals with their acute senses, thus encouraging the animal to 'play up' to a greater degree. This was just one of the reasons we needed to treat Bridget's nervousness.

It's often the case after serious injury that athletes experience fear of their chosen sport, even though they are fully aware that nothing has changed. Their bodies have set up an unconscious mechanism to guide them away from perceived dangers. Without the self-image of being the competent rider Bridget had previously experienced she found her private life difficult to handle. We worked on cognitive behavioural responses that would show that she had alternative choices in the future if for any reason riding ceased to be an option for her. It is undesirable for athletes to run their whole lives under the guise of sports accomplishments, when gone, there emerges a void, their self image and confidence then suffers. Together we were able to find new acceptable activities to immerse Bridget in when not riding or looking after the animals. She developed the other areas of her life, although horses remained a large aspect in this equation.

Bridgets riding climbed back to its former level within days of therapy. We continued using suggestion therapy for a number of weeks which helped Bridget to understand and utilise self-hypnosis a little better for the resolution of future problems. I also acted in a life coaching capacity, helping Bridget to create the life she really desired. Once outside influences and social pressure to conform are eliminated, it is often interesting to note the extent at which people begin to achieve their desires. What their parents might think; being regarded as 'different' by society or conforming to rules are common influences that trouble people. It is often the case that people excel in their chosen careers when they finally throw off the shackles and decide to do the things they want to do. Those things they truly value in life. The sad thing is this transformation rarely occurs before their fourth or fifth decade, leaving less time to really enjoy their lives as they want them.

Chapter Six

Hypnotic Inductions
—*making the connection.*

"When you become quiet, it just dawns on you"

—Edison.

Effectual Inductions
—*the Parasympathetic systems natural escalator.*

Inductions have already been covered to some degree in the previous chapter. We have discovered what they are (the narrowing of consciousness) but we have yet to explain what possible content lies within a hypnotic induction.

A skilful hypnotist will have a number of inductions at his disposal and is able to create new effective scripts at will. Everyone is unique to some extent, therefore reacts slightly differently in different situations, for this reason alone the hypnotist needs to remain flexible in his approach.

Hypnotists should always tell their subjects about the internal and external experiences that are going to happen, this is the art of hypnosis. Two effects are seen from this, one; it helps to convince the hypnotic that something is occurring and two; it builds confidence in the abilities of the hypnotist. The physiological response from taking three deep breaths is a higher level of oxygen in the blood, due to increased breathing. This in turn constricts blood vessels to the brain causing a feeling of slight dizziness. The subject will respond by believing something is happening due to hypnosis.

Such demonstration acts as a way to alter even the most sceptical person's perceptions of reality. This combination of fact, physiological responses and compounding of suggestions serves as a potent cocktail in the hypnotist's armoury. There are many, many examples of these mixtures of physiological and psychological combinations and they are only restricted by the practitioner's imagination.

Another element frequently found in hypnotic inductions is the addition of water scenarios. It is assumed that all human beings have relaxation responses associated with water and the act of floating. This is predominantly due to humans associating water with the once immersion in amniotic fluids in their mothers womb. The many inductions incorporating, 'going deeper down a staircase', 'travelling through a warm tunnel gradually getting colder and seeing trees at the end of the tunnel' are all unconscious analogies in order to reinstate the pleasant environment of the unborn child graduating to birth.

One of the best ways I feel to choose an induction is through empathy. Notice a type of induction that just somehow feels good, one you are simply attracted to.

I have set out some guidelines for inducing hypnosis in this chapter, but there is no reason why you should not change them or even make up your own. Have a look at the scripts and try to decipher the underlying reasons for the themes and elements in them, this will enable you to gain a greater understanding of how to build your own. When it comes down to it, it really does not matter about including long elaborate tales in inductions, the key point is to create a level of relaxation. The simplest way to do this is to close your eyes and to gradually relax your body one part at a time, including some soft non-repetitive music in this equation will enhance the benefits. Inductions are essentially quick ways of accessing this state and are very good methods of deepening the level of hypnosis. So just give a few a go and find the ones which work best for you, and enjoy the process, it is fun. For best results it is often preferable to tape your inductions and scripts on to tape or c.d. as this allows further relaxation. Many people find that it's hard to relax whilst listening to their own voice, so get a friend to record it for you. Alternatively you can buy ready made cd's from my website address at the back of this book.

Index of Inductions

1. Quick Double Eye Fixation Method.
2. Staircase Method.
3. Eye Fixation Method.
4. Balloon Ride Induction.
5. Deepening the State of Hypnosis.
6. Autogenic Muscle Relaxation Induction.

1-Quick Double Eye Fixation Method.

Begin by sitting in straight back chair.

Close your eyes and take in a few deep breaths, relax with each breath that you take.

I will then count from three down to one. On the count of one your eyes will close again and your whole body will feel loose and limp. You will quickly enter a Hypnotic sleep.

Now open your eyes and try to keep them open until I reach the number one.

Three, your eyes are feeling heavy and drowsy.

Two, nearly there, your eyes will close on the count of one.

One, eyes close and sleep.

Now let the muscles around your eyes relax completely, that's good.

Allow your shoulders to drop back.

Your eyes become so relaxed, you are no longer able or willing to open them. It feels so good to be here, so relaxed.

As you breathe in, your body may relax even further and as that breath is released your eyes double their relaxation, and this continues.

Let every muscle become loose and limp as if you were asleep, legs and arms limp, shoulders relaxed, jaw slightly open and r-e-l-a-x-e-d.

It's so calm and peaceful, you just sit there knowing there is nothing expected of you except to relax.

2-Staircase Method.

In a moment I'm going to count down from ten to one, when I say the word ten you will allow your eyes to gently shut.

Number Ten close your eyes now.

And as they close you will begin to imagine a movie screen inside your mind, an imaginary staircase appears on a screen at the top of the inside of your forehead.

This is a movie screen that plays your thoughts and feelings. The movie will display a large wide stone staircase leading down to a beautiful, country garden.

The sun is beaming down on the garden, in the middle is a small shallow pond with a fountain trickling away in the middle. There is a wonderful drooping willow tree in the corner with birds high up in its branches, you can hear them sing. You pleasantly admire the calming, peacefulness of the garden.

Such a peaceful place.

(Leave gap to visualise)

When I say the number nine, you are still at the top of those stairs leading to the garden in your mind. In a moment you will step down those stone steps, and as I continue to count down to one, you will progressively go down until you reach this beautiful country garden.

Each number will bring with it double the previous numbers level of relaxation. On the number One you will be deeper in relaxation than you have ever been, your body will be relaxed but your mind will be alert and focused on your desired goal.

Number 9—Double that relaxation now.
Number 8—Deeper and deeper.
Number 7—Down those stairs one at a time.
Number 6—Down, down, deeper. imagine yourself breathing in calmness.
Number 5—Relaxing even more, more than before.

Number 4—Calm and peaceful, nothing to do except to relax.
Number 3—Double that previous relaxation.
Number 2—Almost all the way down to calmness.
Number 1—And completely relaxed and at ease.

A calm and peaceful garden is yours, you allow yourself to drift even closer to that goal by walking slowly to the willow tree in the corner of the garden. The branches shade you from the hot sun as you sit beneath this tree in awe of your beautiful surroundings. You sink comfortably into the soft, green, grass. Such a wonderful feeling to be here, it's a place that in your mind you always knew was there, it's a place you knew you could reach with a little effort.

You let your thoughts just wander, as I give you suggestions to assist you in the attainment of your desires.

These suggestions will be accepted by your unconscious mind and acted upon, because you know they are for your wellbeing, its true.

(Add Suggestions or deepener)

3-Eye Fixation Method.

This is one of the traditional ways of inducing hypnosis. The method once used by hypnotists who swung a pocket watch in front of the hypnotic's eyes, causing a feeling of drowsiness and eye heaviness. The main object of this induction is to focus ones gaze at a given object on a fixed point in the room and to keep that gaze throughout.

By observing the physical reaction, one can intensify the results. For example if you feel that your eyes are becoming very tired and you'd like to close them, hold them in the opened position a little longer, then close them and notice the pleasure and intense feeling of relief and relaxation. Dwell on this relaxation and increase it. Noticing one's internal dialogue will help, try to steer it into a direction of relaxation.

Fix your gaze on an object, something shiny such as a diamond, piece of reflective glass or candle flame is effective. Notice its movements, the reflections, colours and shadows.

Take three deep breaths, as you continue to focus on the object, try not to blink. Eyes tend to dry up quickly when one ceases to blink and the lids become heavy. That's alright its perfectly OK.

You focus on the object before you, keeping your eyes wide open. Notice the colours and the reflections, in particular notice the colour blue, the blue reflections of light.

Your focus has the effect of making you physically tired, but this does not stop you from continuing.

The longer you stare the heavier your eye lids become, the deeper the level of relaxation you will achieve. Drowsier and drowsier, in a moment you may allow your eyelids to gently drop, remain focused.

It's getting harder and harder to keep awake, when your eyes do finally close, you can step into a beautiful, peaceful deep level of relaxation. Where your eyes can relax.

Getting heavier and heavier, slowly closing, and tightly shut.

Tightly close those eyes and now relax them. You can notice how comfortable this feels to be so relaxed.

This is your time to relax, there is nothing whatsoever for you to do other than to relax.

Calm, relaxed, contented, it's easy for you.

Allow your jaw to open slightly and feel how relaxed it becomes.

And as you continue to breathe gently and progressively relax even further, your mind becomes aware of the suggestions I will make. Each suggestion will be delivered to your unconscious mind and acted upon. Each suggestion will have an effect of relaxing you even further.

(Add suggestions.)

4-Balloon Ride Induction.

Imagine yourself in a wonderful hot air balloon.

You imagine yourself in the basket of the balloon as it is about to be launched, you feel safe and comfortable, there is a feeling of excitement and anticipation in the air.

At last the balloon lifts gently off, taking you up in its basket with a wonderful feeling of freedom and adventure, you are beginning to drift along. You have a quiet confidence about *the changes* that *you will* see.

You can visualise the balloon lift into the air, you are floating, drifting, you are being warmed by the hot sun as you gently gain height.

You start to notice the wonderful sights below you, the reflections of sun on water as you pass a deep blue coloured lake. You notice animals drinking from the fresh clean lake, just drinking what they need, no more, no less but you do notice the beautiful deep blue colour of the water.

Focus on the deep blue colour of the lake, making you even more relaxed, even more relaxed.

Even at this height you notice you are not alone, clouds drift on above you, the warm breeze brushes your face. The landscape below is somehow familiar, you've seen it before, perhaps in life, in a book or in your imagination, but you do feel you have seen this landscape before, and this feels good.

You can feel the benefits on your health of breathing the fresh air as you drift along, slowly, peacefully, contented.

The balloon drifts very slowly, across open fields, passing over many wonderful sights and sounds.

With each breath you take, you find yourself feeling more and more relaxed, each breath brings with it relaxation.

All of the colours of the scenery interest you, you watch in awe.

The sky is filled with the beautiful light of the sun, as the sun starts to sink over the horizon. The sky is filled with a kaleidoscope of colour. So natural, so calming.

The colours begin to develop into a red glow. Concentrate on that red glow as it turns orange. A sky streaked full of many shades of the colour orange. Focus on orange.

The colour yellow now develops, in your own time. The orange glow turns to a deep yellow in colour. There are streaks of colour all across the sky, focus on this colour, now predominately yellow orange.
(Gap)

Drifting along peacefully, the colours slowly continue to change until they merge into a green blue, a green blue fusion of colour.
The sun continues to sink, bringing less light, the sky is almost entirely blue, getting darker. Beautiful. How relaxing this is. Deep blue.

Deep dark blue drifting slowly to purple. Deep purple all the way until the sky eventually develops into the final colour of violet.

Focus on the colour violet. All the way to relaxation now.

All of your previous anxieties and tensions just float away.

With this new level of relaxation you realise the balloon has begun to drift down towards the ground, slowly, gently until it peacefully settles on the ground below, so smoothly, certainly much more gently than you had expected.

You now allow yourself to rest peacefully against the side of the balloons basket, knowing you are safe, very peaceful, very relaxed.

You gently close your eyes and enter a peaceful light sleep, feeling the warm breeze stroke against your face. What a wonderful feeling this is, drifting, gently, peacefully.

Now I'm going to give you those suggestions, and you will act upon them, just let the suggestions drift over you, not accepting or rejecting them, just relax and allow them to flow through you. Your subconscious is able to absorb the suggestions that it feels are most beneficial to your happiness and well being.

(Add suggestions.)

5-Deepening the State of Hypnosis.

Continue to relax as you have done so well already, now we are going to relax even further and you'll feel twice as good as you do now.

You will be physically relaxed but your mind will remain alert to my suggestions.

I want you to count backwards starting with the number one hundred. Every time you say a number, hear it echo in your mind, visualise the numbers actually fading in to the distance, reducing in colour and size until they disappear. The act of counting backwards and hearing the numbers echo in your mind will have the effect of doubling the amount of numbers counted. All the numbers continue to multiply as they fade. This will double your level of relaxation each time you say a number.

You will certainly find that by the time you reach the number eighty, you will be physically relaxed but mentally alert to the suggestions I will give. The numbers will have just faded into the distance, you'll have nothing what-so-ever left to do. You will feel peaceful and calm.

The numbers will have progressively faded away, the numbers will have gone from your mind. If by chance a few numbers remain, just keep counting until they fade away—and they will.

Now start the process, say the number 'One hundred', double your relaxation and hear the number echo in your mind. Doesn't that feel good? Feel your muscles relax.

Continue to say the second number now 'Ninety-nine' and double your relaxation again. The numbers are beginning to fade in to the distance as you carry on counting. Notice how even more relaxed you feel with each number—stepping down.

Now continue to count backwards and on each number double your level of relaxation and multiply the amount of numbers you see. Notice them fade until you reach eighty.

Soon they will all be gone.

(Count backwards)

'Eighty' double that relaxation and all gone—faded. That's good.

You can continue to relax with each breath you take if you choose to, or if you don't.

The numbers are all gone. The numbers have faded away from your mind. They are all gone and you can't find any more numbers. The numbers are all gone from your mind, and your mind as well as your body is relaxed now.

You continue to take notice of my suggestions.

You are more relaxed than you can ever remember being, so relaxed that your conscious mind is going to fade out just like those numbers did.

In a short while I'm going to give you some suggestions for your well being, and because your conscious mind is asleep they will pass straight to your unconscious mind and you will act upon them.

Now I will begin…

6-Autogenic Muscle Relaxation Induction.

Whilst listening to this tape I want you to concentrate only on what is being said, creating a mental picture, role playing in your mind, exactly what is being Visualised.

Do not try too hard to drop into a trance, as you will tense up, just relax and flow with the tape.

If at any time you feel it difficult to follow my instructions, or you fall asleep, that's alright, it's perfectly alright, you are still benefiting from the tape.

Firstly I'd like you to sit comfortably or lay down somewhere quiet and peaceful, somewhere you are unlikely to be disturbed. Turn down the light ,you may wish to wear headphones if that would cut out noise and increase your concentration.

In just a moment, together, we are going to relax your body one part at a time. But first, I want to give you an instruction, that whilst you relax and listen to this tape, if anyone needs you, the phone rings there is an emergency or someone is at the door, you will simply wake up and attend to the situation.

O.K. lets begin by firstly breathing in deeply and relaxing completely, breathe in deeply and slowly release that breath completely, feel your stomach muscles tense as you exhale, and relax—*R-E-L-A-X* your muscles.

As you begin to feel relaxed and at peace, I want you to increase that relaxing sensation in the toes of your feet.
Wiggle your toes and relax your toes.

Feeling the relaxing sensation in your toes wash down into the instep of your feet, slowly washing down to your heals and around your Ankles—*R-e-l-a-x* your ankles. Your feet are totally relaxed.
Moving on down to your Thighs, and completely relax your thigh muscles.
Loose and limp, *l-o-o-s-e and l-i-m-p*. Your legs are totally relaxed.

As your hips relax, the whole of your lower body begins to feel a temperature change and weight change. As you relax you can feel the warmth in your lower body and your legs become either light or heavy, it doesn't matter which, but you do notice whether your lower body becomes heavier in weight or if it is becoming lighter in weight, and that sensation increases.
You can feel the texture of the surface which your body is touching.
How pleasant it is to become so completely relaxed and so at ease. You are relaxed and at ease.

As you breathe in deeply and relax completely I want you to feel the tightness in your stomach muscles, and your stomach muscles relax.

All the tension and anxiety is leaving your body, imagine a warm glow is flowing through your torso, from your lower spine along your back into your chest muscles-Your chest muscles relax.

Let your shoulders drop down, relaxing your shoulders *Down* through to your arms, forearms and fingers—Wiggle your fingers, allow your fingers to relax.

You are relaxed and at ease, your body is going to sleep, but your mind is awake and alert.

Let the sound of my voice send you into an even deeper level of relaxation.
Deeper and deeper down, down, down.

As your neck begins to relax, you allow the heaviness of your head to drop down and relax completely.
Your eyes might be tired by now, so let them rest in a closed position and become tightly shut, tightly shut, that's right.

Allow a little space between your teeth and relax your jaw.

Your whole body relaxes and sinks down, down, down. You are going even deeper into a relaxing level of body and mind.

DEEPER and *DEEPER* as I count backwards from Ten to One, your body is going to sleep.

Number 10, Deeper and deeper down, down.
Number 9, Relaxing going down, down, down.
Number 8, Down, down ,down, relax.
Number 7, Deeper and deeper.
Number 6, Down, down, down.
Number 5, Relaxing your body—relax.
Number 4, Loose and limp, loose and limp.
Number 3, Even further down.

Number 2, Totally relaxed and at ease.

Number 1, You are incredibly relaxed, your body is going to sleep, but your mind is receptive to the suggestions that I make. We have now drawn back the curtains that separate the conscious and unconscious minds, allowing us access to your unconscious mind, to help you make the changes in your mental and physical body, enabling you to achieve your goals. You are very receptive to the life changing suggestions that I will give you.

Chapter Seven

Constructing Scripts for Sport and Life
—*affirmation manifestation.*

'Everything that you say and do is a reflection of the inner you.'
—Successeries Ltd.

Hypnotic Scripts—*lyrics of transformation.*

There are many reasons for the various types of scripts used for hypnotic inductions. Some scripts incorporate stories and tales, some unconscious metaphors that tell a tale. Others are simple suggestions dreamt up by the practitioner which have little real unconscious value. Whichever type of script one uses, the levels of effectiveness can vary from person to person for a multitude of reasons.

The best suggestion I can give for constructing scripts, if one is not an experienced hypnotist, is to keep it simple.

One can dream up elaborate tales which create rich colourful visualisations in the mind, but without a fuller understanding of the mind it might be possible to unconsciously create another story which you did not intend. There is no danger involved in hypnosis, but it might be possible to decrease the effectiveness.

Within a hypnotic script it can be very effective to weave a visual story making it as colourful and vivid as possible. It is interesting to see that research suggests that a visual image does not need to be true to life to have an effect on the body. Let me explain by way of an example.

If one wishes to reduce ones own heart rate at any given time, it can be done in one of two ways. The subject could sit down in a quiet place (which alone will have an effect) and concentrate solely on his or her heart rate, he or she would imagine the heart is reducing in a number of beats per minute. This technique will have an effect and results are likely to be seen.

The other much more effective form of visualising to reduce the heart rate, again involves the subject sitting down somewhere quiet and peaceful, but with the addition that this time he or she visualises a relaxing, calm provoking scene or situation directed in the effort to reduce ones heart rate. Creating a mental picture in your mind of a calm and peaceful place (such as a beach perhaps) has on its own dramatic pacifying effects, but is much more effective if the subject directs his/her mind on achieving a specific goal (reduced heart rate).

The above example is given for the purpose of demonstrating that when visualising in order to develop a goal, it is far more effective to direct a vivid image with colour and sound towards a specific task, rather than just at the desired result.

If trying to do the opposite of increasing the heart rate one would direct the mind to do so, whilst simultaneously thinking of a fast, exciting scenario, thus increasing the effectiveness.

As I mentioned earlier, these visualisations need not be real or accurate in detail. You can see some examples of this in my scripts later in this book. Lets take the example of cancer patients who have proved in some recent studies to have tremendous results in fighting their disease through meditation or self-hypnosis.

Patients are often told that if they go into a state of self-hypnosis and to visualise their cancer cells being fought off by their immune system then this helps their bodies do just that. In the majority of cases, patients have little or no knowledge of what a cancer cell or indeed much of their complicated internal system looks like. This is not a problem, clearly it would be most inappropriate to expect these people to complete a doctorate in medicine! Instead they are left to imagine in anyway they wish to, that the cancer cells in the diseased body part is being fought successfully by whatever they choose to imagine. In some cases, the patient visualises vivid networks of cogs and switches in their bodies just like a robot or a bionic physique perhaps. As long as the psyche is directed towards a specific goal, told what the end result is to be and a system of visualisation is put into place. The positive effects are dramatic, remember the unconscious mind has no logic or reasoning facility, it merely accepts information or directions as given.

An interesting point about affirmations is that a negative one always takes root in the subconscious. This means if the sports person tells themself that they may fail or trip at the final hurdle and this is backed up by visualisation then in all probability they will. This is partially due to the fact that negative self-talk often has strong emotions attached to it, these break through into the unconscious mind more readily.

Unfortunately positive suggestions are not always so efficient, this is why an altered state is used, it increases ones chances of success dramatically.

Always be positive, I don't know about you but I don't want negative affirmations fed into my psyche if possible. A quote well used today by well meaning corporate managers is 'Failure is not an option'. This to me is a mistake, why even mention failure? It only acts to create a mental picture in peoples minds that failure is possible, surely a better version would be; 'Success is inevitable'.

I mention this because one still needs to be aware of the fact that there are indirect commands in both the English language and even more so under the microscope of Hypnosis. If I said the above affirmation in another context I might say 'Success is the only option', this sounds positive, and of course it is. But just look at the connotations, we still need to make sense of its meaning. To know that success is the only option we sometimes need to verify that by being aware of the other options, which in this case is failure. Gets confusing doesn't it? Lets look at a simpler example. Let's say I want you to *not* think of the colour blue. Now to process that information you must first visualise or at least understand the meaning of the colour blue. This is clearly the opposite of what I required, I wanted you *not* to think of blue and in that statement I essentially directed you to do so (albeit unconsciously). So it is necessary to be aware of what you are both telling someone to do and what you are not telling someone to do! The reason being is that you need to process the information in someway to make sense of it. This can work to your advantage in some forms of hypnosis due to your ability to direct someone to act indirectly, and as they process the information it is consciously missed and only processed at an unconscious level. A very useful tool in Hypnosis.

When constructing scripts try to add as many sensory experiences as possible. Describe what you would see, hear and feel in the situation. Listen to the applause of the crowds, take notice of how your friends and family will react on your fine performance. Feel how you would stand and hold your body, the tension in your muscles as you deliver that perfect shot perhaps—make it real!

Finally, when you have finished the session of hypnosis you might like to come out again to full consciousness and to get on with your everyday life, alternatively you may wish to carry on into sleep if it is time to go to bed. I add the following text to my scripts which tend to cover most occurrences;

"As we come to the end of this tape, I want you to do one of two things."

"If you are in bed ready to go to sleep, then simply continue to go into a nice deep sleep, until you are required to awaken. If you are not about to go to sleep for the night, then when I count up from 5—1 wake up feeling energetic, refreshed and extremely pleased with your ongoing success."

5—Coming on up now.
4—Starting to awaken, that's right.
3—Coming on up now, good.
2—Open your eyes.
1—Wide-awake—Wide-awake, feeling good.

Kate, Basketball player—Case study 5.

An example of the ability to subconsciously direct oneself to fail in the sporting arena is the concept that a person is unable to complete a task at a competent level on more than one occasion, in a single session. Let me give you an example, her name was Kate, although she was an International Hockey player, surprisingly she approached me about her basketball skills at University level.

Kate's hockey was her 'main' sport, certainly it was the game she went to University to pursue, Basketball was her way of relaxing. However over the last few months something in her game had become disjointed, which stopped her enjoyment as she felt she was letting the rest of the team down. It was no longer a game of relaxation but frustration.

The problem was that in match games Kate was the predominant basket taker (free throws) if the team approached the scoring area. This was fine, Kate enjoyed the opportunity to excel, the aspect that was troubling her was the fact that she was often expected to take a succession of shots all in a short period of time.

Fine I said what's the problem? "Well, you can't get a basket every time in succession, can you?" "Why not?" I inquired? "The law of averages, I suppose?" She replied! Apparently, and I have found this to be a problem in almost every scoring sport, it's perfectly acceptable to take a shot at a basket (for example) and to get the ball in on the first shot. But if you take ten shots for instance, then the majority will not go in. Kate explained this concept to me in detail. So I asked whether it was possible to come to the gym on ten separate occasions and take one shot each day, and get that shot into the net every single time? Well, yes that did seem to be possible in Kate's mind. So, the upturn of this idea is that, a sports person can get a direct shot one or two times, sometimes up to five times out of ten, but it is unacceptable to be able to get every single shot out of ten, well, certainly not during the same session. Initially this amazed me when I first heard such a story. In my mind it's clear that the physical external aspects of the game always remain the same, how then is it not possible to get every shot if one is skilled enough to get the first or second? The answer is in the mind. It is a fault that our society programmes us to believe, it is the law of averages, when in reality, it's just up to us. Surely you might miss some, but you don't have to!

I agreed to work with Kate using hypnosis to eliminate this mental block and to release her potential. This was fairly simple and only took one session, mainly on the grounds that she was an accomplished athlete and had confidence in her abilities. The other major aspect was that Kate had many good quality past references to back her self up as being a winner.

The main focus in this sort of problem is internal dialogue (usually a major factor in the rising of this problem) and concentration. The focus on past success was able to evoke some extra confidence in Kate and some added positive suggestions were also applied. I taught Kate to notice the self-talk that she communicated to herself and to eliminate doubt by changing this for the positive.

Another aspect that one almost always needs to undertake is to watch the player in their sporting environment and to notice differences in their play. The times in which they are successful compared to when they are unsuccessful. This might be a physiological style difference or a mental one.

Kate was soon back on track with her shots, and reluctantly admitted that it was true that perhaps ten baskets out of ten in succession was a possibility, and proved this to be the case.

Hypnotic Scripts Index.

1. Athletic Smoking Cessation.
2. Boxing Power.
3. Breast Enhancement.
4. Endless Endurance.
5. Exceptional Golf.
6. Martial Arts Spiritual Development.
7. Rugby Football.
8. Silky Soccer Skills.
9. Sports Fear Control.
10. Sports Success Programming.
11. Style Improvement.
12. Supreme Weight loss.
13. Top Level Tennis.
14. Weight Gain for Bodybuilding.

Athletic Smoking Cessation

'It's easy to give yourself excuses for not stopping.'
— Uri Geller's Mind-Power Book. Virgin publishing.

Introduction

Sports and smoking do not go hand in hand! It's almost inconceivable that anybody smokes in this day and age let alone the athlete. Smoking is extremely easy to stop if the right tools are utilised. 'Will power' is the most common technique but many people find they lack the strength. As seen in this book, motivation is relatively easy to strengthen and techniques have been discussed in the previous chapters. We know that if we can reinforce our goals with enough reasons we can motivate ourselves to do anything.

A survey carried out by the 'New Scientist Magazine' which surveyed over 72000 smokers found that Hypnosis was the most effective form of smoking cessation over every other method.* Will power had a success rate of only six percent. There are many reasons for this, I believe that one of the strongest is hypnotherapy's ability to access the unconscious mind where behaviours originate. If a person was capable of consciously altering their behaviour then that individual would do so. It's clear to all who smoke that it is dangerous and has no real benefits at an intellectual level.

This means that there must be unconscious forces at play, otherwise this conscious reasoning would prevail and the intelligent being would cease doing this irrational activity.

It's interesting to see that people find it amazingly easy to give up smoking or over eating if they have a compelling enough reason to change. With the smoker often it takes an illness or the development of a nasty cough to decide that perhaps his health has deteriorated enough. Finally realising that he is not immune to the black tar that he 'enjoys' inhaling. It's somewhat frustrating when people claim that nicotine is very addictive, but at the same time other people can decide to give up smoking in an instant and stay off the drug forever. Humans all have the same neurology, how can it be addictive to one but not the other? Because it's not a substance addiction but a mental and behavioural one, force of will can prevail, the studies on hypnosis show this. Hypnosis works on the unconscious mind so 'will power' is required to a lesser degree. If you need help from an expert, go and get the help. If you can't do it by yourself then seek help, it's as simple as that, stop making excuses.

Some of the key benefits of smoking cessation are that in only four days all traces of nicotine will be gone from your body, it's both encouraging and motivational to notice these benefits as one goes along.

Drinking water to help remove nicotine and poisons from your system is beneficial too. It also helps to have an activity such as getting a glass of water to initially replace the nervous activity that used to be smoking a cigarette. As nicotine leaves your body, the sugar level in your blood also drops, this causes the craving for nicotine. Eating oranges or grapefruit in the next four days will prevent the sugar cravings. After these four days you will no longer feel any cravings for nicotine, any subsequent cravings are behavioural ones which will be dealt with by hypnosis. Because smoking is a nervous habit, you may feel stress, take Vitamin B complex for ten days.

The interesting point many of my clients have pointed out to me is that just because you have a craving does not mean you have to react to it. Just as with the weight control patient, hunger does not always have to be a signal to eat, its not an agonising pain, hunger is merely a uncomfortable signal, it can become quite a pleasant feeling if one wishes to view it that way. The same goes for smoking cessation. The craving can signal to you consciously a feeling of pride and pleasure in your ability to give up, it's a signal of mental strength and will power. You could congratulate yourself on a wonderful accomplishment, rather than beat yourself up for not allowing yourself another. A final point before starting your suggestions is to make clear that a powerful tool to any change is to realise that you need to develop your self-image to coincide with your new life style. It is not good enough to merely decide that you are now giving up smoking or trying to give up. When a person is a non-smoker they do not smoke, no questions. That means they do not have even one cigarette a week, one a fortnight or one a year. The option is not there, a non-smoker does not have any cigarettes because they do not smoke. Cut off that option, cease making excuses why you could just have one because you are stressed or it is a special occasion, your lungs do not understand that special occasions are times when they are not allowed to develop cancer. So a way to help this is to view yourself in a different light, as a sports person this should be easy. What sort of person do you think you need to be to change from a smoker to a non-smoker? What aspects do you need to focus on? These are your personal decisions, as an athlete perhaps decide that you are more committed to health and sports excellence, than smoking. Which is true, isn't it?

Something you may like to add to the following script is a form of aversion therapy. It is based on making a person reject a thought or behaviour by making it feel very unpleasant. In weight loss one might focus on the fat in food, the stodgy unpleasant sight of fatty white lard, for example. With smoking cessation you would focus upon the acrid, black tar substance blocking your clean pink airways. The disgusting burning black tar taste that needs to travel through your mouth, reducing your ability to taste food, and breathe correctly. Your blood is poisoned by these strong anti oxygen substances that travel and block up the veins throughout your body, reducing your sports performance. How do you think your sports performance will develop when you stop smoking?

*Survey carried out by Frank Schmidt of Iowa University and published in the 'New Scientist' Magazine and the 'Journal of Applied Psychology'.

Script

You quit smoking forever, it's true you are a healthy non-smoker.

You find that you have more control over your life, over your thoughts and feelings, more control over your sporting accomplishments. And from this day on things just get better and better, it's easy for you.

I want you to continue to relax, both now and in life in general. You're going to find something that you thought was going to be difficult turns out to be ridiculously easy and carries on getting easier and easier with each day that goes by.

You're going to find yourself taking a lot of pride and a lot of pleasure in the ease at which you quit smoking, and how effective it has been in increasing your sporting performance. You will notice the results.

The benefits you are already gaining from smoking cessation are immense, and they continue to get better and better as days go by.

If you play sports your smoking is affecting your performance.

As an athlete you no longer have the need to buy cigarettes, but if you are offered one you will feel a surge of pride and confidence and the thought "I'm an athlete, I don't smoke" will appear in your mind. Those words just come to you in your mind, "I'm an athlete I don't smoke".

And you find yourself taking a lot of pride and a lot of pleasure in knowing that you are a health conscious athlete "I'm an athlete I don't smoke".

Smoking has hindered your athletic performance in the past, "I'm an athlete I don't smoke".

You quit the habit of smoking forever. You are a healthy non smoker.
You feel you have more control over your life, over your thoughts and behaviours, more control over your sporting accomplishments.

From this day on things just get better and better, it's easy for you.

The benefits you are already gaining from smoking cessation are immense, and these get better and better.

You realise smoking has hindered your athletic performance in the past, so you correct this, "no thanks, I'm an athlete"

And you're going to find yourself taking a lot of pride and a lot of pleasure in the ease at which you quit smoking, and how effective it has been in increasing your sporting performance.

You're going to find something that you thought was going to be difficult is ridiculously and unbelievably simple. You have more control over your behaviour and more control over your mind than you thought possible. You command yourself to regain control.

You are a health conscious athlete, as for smoking, it's a dirty habit you used to have. You feel more calm more relaxed than before.

You feel more calm, more confident.

Your lungs become cleaner, fresher, much more efficient at their job. You have a new sense of vitality.

Your breathing becomes clearer, fresher and easier. Your physical activities improve as a result.

What a nasty, dirty habit it has become to you.
You quit smoking, that's right, you lose that habit for good.

And you find that you do quit smoking. You find you take a lot of pride and a great deal of pleasure in the ease with which you give up smoking.

You'll find it surprises you and it amazes you but at the same time it gives you a lot of pride and confidence at the ease of which you quit smoking. And you tell your friends how easy it was through Hypnosis.

You realise the damage you would be doing if you were still a smoker, I wonder how long it will take you to notice that you have already begun to change, but not as much as by tomorrow.

You will find now that you have quit smoking, there is a reduction of nicotine in your system, and with this absence of nicotine, you feel a much calmer, confident feeling, and this feeling will persist and stay with you.

Smoking is a dirty habit you used to have.

You have more money to spend, you have more energy and vitality to do the things you want to do. You are now able to breathe more easily, and your fitness is increasing, all due to smoking cessation.

What a wonderful feeling.

Regain control.

You have stopped smoking quickly and easily, much easier than you thought possible. This time it was easy, you know this, it's true. You have stopped smoking, and you have stopped smoking for the rest of your life.

You gain a lot of pride and a great deal of pleasure from the positive comments you receive from your friends about ceasing the habit of smoking, and you tell you friends how easy it was through Hypnosis, because it was easy, much easier than you thought.

The process to cleanse your body has started, now that you have quit the harmful habit of smoking.

Imagine

Imagine a time when you have given up the habit of smoking, imagine the athletic benefits you are going to be able to attain with your new found strength, vitality, easy breathing. You can feel how easy your breathing has become.

You appreciate good quality foods more because of your quest for health and new found sense of taste.

A feeling of excitement saturates your body because you realise now that your sense of taste and smell is more important to you than smoking ever was.

You feel fitter, healthier and much, much more confident in all the areas of your life, due to this new found freedom.

You have quit the habit of smoking for the rest of your life, and it feels good.

You visualise your self in your chosen sport, you are breathing with ease. It amazes you at how much better you feel whilst exercising. Your stamina and fitness have increased dramatically, and this improves your performance no end. You are less out of breath than when you smoked. You feel a great sense of pride and satisfaction because you feel so good to be so health conscious. You decide to stop smoking for the rest of your life.

You have stopped smoking.

Now I want you to direct your lungs to kick-start the process of returning to the healthy condition of a non-smoker. Your body is now directed to cleanse your lungs of impurities and eliminate any former health problems. This process is on super power.

Picture your clean airways, the tubes to the lungs are clear and healthy. Your breathing is free and easy. You can picture fresh clear blood cells circulating the vessels and cells of the lungs, these blood cells attack and clear away any final deposits of black tar or pollutants in every healthy way possible.

Your lungs are functioning completely, they are producing new clear, healthy lung cells in replace of the old polluted ones.

You notice that you are far less anxious in everyday life and a lot more confident.

And as I am quiet for a while I want you to consider silently in your own mind, some of the benefits you are going to experience now you have stopped smoking for good.

OK, begin ...

(leave gap)

Now that we are coming to the end of this session, I'm going to count from One to Five, on the count of Five you will wake up feeling good, because you have already achieved a great deal.

1. Becoming aware of the everyday sounds around you.
2. Coming up now to consciousness.
3. You feel fresh and full of energy.
4. Almost completely awake, that's good.
5. *WIDE AWAKE.*

Boxing Power

▼

'I'm gonna be champ. I'm the kind of guy, I just have to get to the threshold. Sometimes it's just difficult getting to the threshold. Once I'm there and I'm in the dressing room the night of the fight, I know I can't be denied.'
—Mike Tyson—Total Sport magazine,
April 1996, interview by Steve Farhood.

Introduction

There is a vast array of varied emotions and qualities required to enter a Boxing ring. To an outsider it might seem difficult to comprehend the complexity of the sport, for a spectator it is far too easy to view boxing as a violent, aggressive sport with little skill involved.

Boxing is one of the most physically and mentally taxing sports available and certainly it requires a unique skill-set to compete at any level. In few sports do you need to battle with fear, pain, adrenaline, and a flurry of punches whilst also remaining level headed enough to read the opponent, enabling yourself to counter their movements effectively.

Boxing is one of the few martial arts where you have to back up technique and theory with real 'full contact' experience.

Boxing is a sport that incorporates many different styles, therefore writing a universal script for all Boxers is difficult. I have put together many of the most frequently seen problems and incorporated them into the following script. If you feel some of the statements are not right for you, then, as with all scripts, it's up to you to develop them for your own needs, view these scripts as a template. Change the scripts when another aspect of your training is in need of manipulation.

Script

Your instinct for your opponents' weaknesses and favourite moves makes you a powerful opponent.

Endurance and strength are based in the mind, you have that power of mind, you have the required focus to complete your task, it's yours, that's true.

You develop your own arousal level to perfection, fear is your ally backed up by courage and action.

You take command of the centre of the ring, you dominate, it's yours to guard.

Your footwork is swift, balanced and poised. You move in short, gliding steps keeping your opponent lined up for sharp punches.

You deliver your arsenal of combinations whenever your opponent loosens his guard.

You have the ability to deliver damaging manoeuvres.

You move around the ring with ease whilst keeping that dominance in the centre of the ring.

Your lead Jab sets-up a cluster of beautiful, dynamic and firm punches that hit and punch through the intended target.

You consistently hit and avoid being hit.

A firm stance enables you to deliver a combination of punches whilst keeping your balance.

You keep your guard high and your chin low at all times.

Your workload is far greater than your opponents.

Your defence is secure and tight.

Your confident body language in and out of the ring drives fear into your opponent.

Your foot positions allow you to measure your distances perfectly.

Get in close when you get the opportunity, this will allow you to deliver devastating hooks and uppercuts.

Powerful counter punches to the body, these are effective for you.

With your speed you deflect jabs easily.

Be prepared to counter at any opportunity.

You are ready for the unexpected.

Move swiftly whenever your opponent is ready to punch, you move with ease.

If you are at any stage overwhelmed by punches, cover up briefly until you notice an opportunity to take back control with a counter attack, do this with calm confidence.

You are dictating this fight on your terms.

Dictate the fight on your terms, this is your fight to win.

Always keep trying.

Pressurise your opponent, increase your workload during the last ten seconds of each round.

Being relaxed at all times increases your reaction times and makes you swift.

You realise your qualities for success and use them to their fullest.

Circle your opponents' blind side to unleash surprise attacks.

Your adrenaline is under control.

You are a skilled, strategic, tactically poised and a physically supreme athlete.

You are a winner.

You accomplish all of your goals.

You are a points accumulator. You deliver twice as many punches as your opponent.

You parry and deflect punches with ease.

Slipping punches and snapping back ready to counter are sharp movements in your repertoire.

Your infighting is tight and aggressive.

You are a smooth operator, you have strategy, tactics, skill, endurance, speed, calmness, courage and the energy to carry out your ambitions.

Your training has paid off, this gives you the confidence you need.

Keep your opponent under pressure, make him do the work. Circle his blind side.

You have all the qualities of success inside you.

Speed is in your hands and foot movements. You have the rapid reactions of a cat.

Explosive movements, strength, muscle power, and a high degree of technical knowledge make you a formidable opponent.

You become more positive with each bout that you have.

You are clear of your motivations and ambitions and these install determination in your attitude. Far more than before.

Imagine

Imagine a fighter that you admire, one that has a similar style to your own. Imagine that he has given you his abilities and talents for the night. What would that feel like? How would people see you? How would your opponent feel stepping into the ring? How would your body feel to move in that manner? What tactics would your mind bring into the fight for you?

Continue this imagination to the successful completion of the fight, make it real.

Once you have done this, do it again make sure you are inside this imaginative body, feeling, hearing, seeing, tasting. Feel what it's like to have the crowd behind you when you win, the admiration, the excitement, the sense of achievement.

Breast Enhancement

▼

'Our body is the feedback mechanism, mirroring to us the quality of our choices of thought, feeling, emotion, breath, nutrients, and movement, and our honouring of life.'
—Gregg Braden, The Isaiah Effect.

Introduction

Female breast development is another area where a considerable amount of research related to enhancement hypnosis can be found. Again a cross over of child like perceptions and attitudes into adult life can be seen causing unnecessary stress and anxiety.

All women have a history for breast manipulation to some degree. They know the growing feeling, the changes in hormonal and physical condition. Breast size increases during sex, menstruation and when gaining weight develops a certain degree of broad mindedness in the female's self-image of what her body can achieve and confirms that results of breast manipulation are possible.

There are well documented increases in breast enhancement of one and a half to two inches in a matter of a just a few weeks. Studies have shown two main contributing factors in female breast enhancement. *One*; the persons concept of her own ability and imaginations. *Two*; the manipulation through hypnosis and removal of mental blocks to growth, such as desires to remain boyish in looks through unconscious motivations.

The perception in girls with the small breast problem often stems from the days when they were (and sometimes still are) regarded as 'daddy's girl'. They exist in a sheltered environment. After the young girl grows up and finds her new 'daddy' in the form of a boyfriend the role is again played out this time by the partner. Subconsciously these women enjoy the benefits associated with the protective treatment they receive, strengthened by the fear of losing the dependency of the partner. The psyche sees no reason to develop 'full' adult breast's in the women whilst the message is consistently sent communicating that she has not fully grown up yet. Add this to the psyches knowledge that her body has still not lost its boyish looks, lacking the curves of a woman and we witness a formidable opponent to the females fight with her self-image.

Restricted breast size can be quite a problem for the self-image of a female. Confidence can be reduced and self-esteem lowered. This evidence is obvious by the number of females opting for painful (emotional, financially and physically) breast surgery. Hypnosis is often used in these cases to 'turn on' mental switches enhancing the growth process, usually having quick and dramatic results.

The hypnotic process in breast enlargement is similar to the 'weight gain for bodybuilding' scripts in that blood flow and hormones are increased, feelings are focused on size, shape, weight and warmth. A tingling sensation is often experienced during the 'trance' when the blood flow increases. The following script outlines many of the main attributes used in hypnotic breast size enhancement.

Script

Imagine a piping hot towel wrapped around your chest, feel the warm, heavy feeling of your breasts as they fill with blood. Notice the tingling sensation, imagine the new shape, weight and feel that you would have with larger breasts.

Direct your body to grow.

Your body already knows what to do, how to turn that switch on releasing those hormones responsible for breast development. It is a simple process to turn that switch on in your mind, the switch responsible for the complex biological changes that have already begun to occur. The switch is also responsible for your health and well being.

I don't know how long it will take for you to notice the changes that have already begun, the changes in your self-image, the changes in your body at a cellular level? But that's OK.

Blood flow increases to the breasts bringing with it growth hormones responsible for increased breast size and the general health of your body.

You have now begun to realise the mental limitations you have set for yourself, and from this new perspective you release these limitations to your development at night in your sleep.

Perhaps you have decided to release those unconscious motivations that encourage your breasts to remain smaller than they were intended to be. Perhaps you had felt a little self-conscious, uneasy or embarrassed by those physical and emotional changes all those years ago. That was when you turned off the switch responsible for your natural womanly development. You now reverse that decision. You now allow yourself to develop fully as nature originally intended, your breasts are allowed to grow in size and shape, as was meant to be.

You can reach your potential.

With each day that passes you are becoming healthier in body and mind. Your self-esteem improves, your confidence is getting better and better.

Imagine still that warm hot towel wrapped around your breasts, imagine the increase in blood flow to your breasts, the increase in size and weight as blood fills your breasts fully. They feel heavy, warm and healthy, such a wonderful feeling.

See yourself as you would like to be, experience the feelings of warmth and heaviness in your breasts. Imagine the confidence you would have with this new curvaceous figure. Imagine the reactions of your family, friends and especially your partner, what a wonderful feeling.

Direct your body to grow.

And with each day that passes your breast development increases until they have reached their full potential. They grow upwards and outwards, your health and well being increases with each day that passes. Your confidence grows, your energy and vitality increases in every way. You are getting better and better, healthier more relaxed.

You have the power of imagination, your body already knows what to do, it knows how to increase your breast size in a positive, healthy manner.

You can now release the hormonal and physiological changes associated with this increase.

I don't know how long it will take for you to notice the difference in your breasts, but you will be very pleased with the results.

Imagine a piping hot towel wrapped around your chest.

Direct your mind to remove all limitations.

Your achievements in your physical body are limited only by your own concept of your abilities and you now re-evaluate your perceptions to assist you in your goal.

Remove all mental blocks to assist you in rapid breast development, you are an adult with adult proportions.

This feeling of warmth and heaviness in the breasts is an increase in blood bringing nourishment and growth hormone to that area.

All hormonal and physiological changes required for healthy increases in breast development are switched on tonight in your sleep and every night until your breasts reach the size and shape you wish them to be.

Your immune system is getting stronger, your skin beams with energy and vitality, everyday you get better and better.

Imagine

Stay still for a while as you imagine once again your breasts at their new size and shape, the feeling of warmth, heaviness and the tingling sensation as they grow with each day that passes.

Hormones are drawn to the area in your sleep, imagine the hormones flowing in the veins and capillaries of your breasts.

Imagine the reactions you will have from family, friends and particularly your partner at how wonderful your breasts have become. You have a new sense of womanly curves, fully developed breasts.

Notice how confident you become in your everyday life.

Endless Endurance

▼

'You can develop mental techniques to keep warm in a cold bath or to prevent panic setting in during a treadmill test when you think you cannot keep going. In long endurance races the same principle applies…
    –Fit for Life—Reach your personal best and stay there.
    By Ranulph Fiennes. Publisher: Little, Brown and Company.

Introduction

Endurance is an accumulation of consistent, stamina based training of the body and powerful self-talk of the mind. Although it is becoming evident that the body now seems capable of developing different levels of fast and slow twitch muscle fibres, dependent upon the type of exercise one regularly partakes in. It is still impossible to make fast developments in training through these methods. Changes in muscle fibre type is extremely slow, running into months and years rather than weeks. For this reason alone one should not only concentrate on gradual, consistent development of physical muscular endurance training but the mental stamina that is required in elite competition. Endurance athletes require a greater percentage of slow twitch muscle fibre which is predominately aerobic (oxygen burning) with a lower heart rate level.

Ninety percent of endurance is based in the mind; you have this power of mind within you. Hypnosis has the ability to re-focus and draw out this power.

To increase endurance it is often a good idea to develop mental rehearsals of the activity in question. When the mind is clear of the likely thoughts, feelings and physical conditions which are going to be experienced, your chance of pushing through them is greatly increased. These don't have to be merely imaginary, one can expose themselves directly to the pain one might face. This will have the effect of increasing tolerance to the pain. Similarly if you get used to the sensations and learn to relax then this will have a physical effect of reducing the oxygen intake, thus increasing the chances of success. Maximum aerobic training is one key to increasing the body's ability to tolerate fatigue and increased lactic acid tolerance.

The use of Hypnosis in the run up to an event can have the effect of developing coping strategies when doubts in abilities to 'carry on' are exposed. Having an arsenal of positive suggestions for various occurrences can push one beyond what's usually possible.

Script

Endurance is based in the mind, you have the power of mind to excel in your sport.

The 'will' is far stronger than the body, your mind out stretches your muscles in endurance.

When the going gets tough, your mental determination is switched on.

Take command of your body and mind.

Your clear goals and motivations install determination in you.

You realise your many qualities for success.

You have endless energy. Your dietary preparation before an event enables your body to store the required amount of glycogen in your muscles for top performance.

You now programme stamina in your mind for easy access when required.

You realise your motivations to succeed, and use these to enhance your performance.

You can do anything you put your mind to.

Your prepared suggestions work well for you.

Your hard work and training has paid off for you, this shows in your performance.

You turn on in your mind the switch that regulates the hormones and biochemicals responsible for your athletic stamina, endurance and determination.

Hypertrophy is easy for you.

You can tap your reserves of determination and motivation whenever you need them, and you do.

Imagine

Imagine yourself in a competitive situation where motivation and extra stamina is required for you to excel in your sport.

See, feel and experience the pain you would have. Now turn on that switch that releases the chemicals and mental stamina that you require. Experience that elated sensation that you would have upon feeling the wave of stamina wash over you. A new sense of pride and determination that pushes your performance to new heights.

You are a winner who accomplishes all of your goals.

You can achieve anything that you desire.

Imagine the results that you will achieve, the congratulations of proud family and friends around you.

Exceptional Golf

'If you are caught on a golf course during a storm and are afraid of lightning, hold up a one-iron. Not even God can hit a one-iron.'
—Lee Trevino.

Introduction

Golf is a sport that reacts particularly well to hypnosis and visualisation. One reason being that most golfing errors are simply 'address' inaccuracies easily adjusted through mind control. A golfers address position is the key to his game because it's the foundation of the swinging motion. Another important aspect of golf enhancement is the focus of attention on the 'ball flight direction', both of these points will be dealt with in the following script.

As I have mentioned previously it is always an advantage to consult a professional sports coach when constructing scripts, as this will help you to focus on key areas ripe for development. Hypnosis is far more effective if it focuses upon correcting as few tasks as possible at any given time.

In Golf the 'Waggle' is an important aspect because it serves a good purpose in reducing initial tension before play, using up nervous energy to relax the player. The other aspect is that it enables one to take a little time to visualise exactly what one is trying to achieve. Take this opportunity to go through the motions in your own mind of that perfect shot you wish to achieve. Access the thoughts, feelings, muscle tension and sounds that will accompany the shot. Visualise the reactions of others around you at your successful shot, and your own elated feelings at being supreme.

In Golf your arousal level need only be adjusted slightly, focusing ones attention for only 20 to 30 seconds is enough. It's not an aggressive sport.

A golfer needs to view the game in a similar manner as the Martial Artist in that he should flow with external forces rather than against them. Use the wind speed to arc the ball in a particular direction, don't fight against the wind. Similarly gravity is your ally. Try to hit the ball and you will receive a tense animated swing. Relax and let your whole body create the perfect, relaxed motion. If you concentrate on hitting the ball you will lose much of your natural flow.

Script

Your address position is carefully adjusted, your feet are shoulder width apart, with an even weight distribution. The perfect position is yours.

Your feet and hips control the swing perfectly and the desired result achieved.

When you make your swing your whole mind and body becomes committed to the act of hitting the ball. Your whole body has one aim.

The strength in your thighs work well as the source of power in your swing. Your thighs serve you well. They are strong and powerful, they produce enough energy to create the shot that you require, and it's easy this way.

Your mind is focused on attaining the direction that the ball must achieve to hit its target perfectly.

Notice your head remains steady through the entire back swing, the head only rises at the last moments of the 'follow through', enabling you to watch the ball hit its target with ease, what a wonderful feeling.

When you approach the opportunity to deliver a Putt, accurate play style becomes less important to you. You feel comfortable doing it your own way, that's how you achieve such quality results, relax and enjoy the natural process.

You feel balanced, poised and confident in your putting style, this relaxes you.

You find it easy to achieve an average of one putt per green. It's easy for you, your initial swings are so accurate. Did you hear that? One putt per green is your average.

Whichever line you choose the ball to take, it will follow that line exactly. You choose whether a straight line is best, a fade or a draw, you are to judge and you do so with confidence and clarity.

Your two hands work in unison to achieve the ultimate putt.

Your putting 'follow through' has locomotive like direction, it follows your sense of direction with ease.

Your hand eye co-ordination is developing in a positive manner because of your confident relaxed attitude.

You use practice swings and waggles to visualise your shots and to encourage accurate hand eye co-ordination, and it works for you.

You develop a new sense of 'reading the green', your eyes pick up contours and obstacles to your success. You find with ease the best line for your shot.

Slopes are assessed with a new sense of confidence.

You read the green perfectly with out exception, it becomes easier each time you do it.

Your body language projects confidence to your opponents and this encourages you.

Imagine

Spend a few moments now imagining beginning a game of golf, or beginning a shot that in the past you have found difficulty in perfecting. Do not visualise performing the shot incorrectly, run through the experience as the perfect player. Correct any faults in your game.

Visualise with clarity, your thoughts, feelings, the way your physical body feels as you move. Also notice the sounds, smells, and temperature of your surroundings.
Begin to focus upon your game and completing your perfect shot.
Run all the way through the experience, make it real!

Martial Arts Spiritual Development

'The first law of war is to preserve ourselves and destroy the enemy.'
—Mao Tse-Tung.

Introduction

The benefits of body mind mastery are no more evident than in the field of martial arts. The following script was put together with a view to encompass the spiritual development of the Martial artist and to increase his/her abilities through mind power. Martial arts is a sport that is misinterpreted by many practitioners in that too much focus is placed on techniques and physical manoeuvres. It is internal energy and mind control that are at the forefront of the effective modern day warriors armoury. These techniques will not only transform combat abilities they will calm, relax, and develop emotional stability.

Script

Poise and balance are yours.

You develop your own arousal level to perfection, fear is your ally backed up by courage and action.

The internal energy flow that is yours creates health, harmony and mental assertiveness.

Your combat ability has the effect of generating a peaceful attitude in yourself and others. You are at peace with yourself and the world in general.

You are developing emotional stability.

Defence of yourself is fast and direct. If you are attacked, you flow with your opponent's movements.

You have the ability to sense the strengths and weaknesses of others, and use this to your advantage in combat situations, it's easy for you.

Stamina is based in the mind. You now programme endless stamina in to your subconscious for easy access when required.

You are agile, fit, spontaneous, disciplined and humble in your actions towards others.

Your abdomen is fuelled with internal energy during the night in your sleep.

You are calm but very alert, movements are swift, your mind is still.

Technical form is important to you, but mind control and energy flow are essential in combat, these you are able to develop fully.

Fight your opponent using his strength against him, your will-power will prevail.

You have ultimate poise and balance, beauty and grace.

Your whole life becomes a tranquil haven in touch with yourself and others. Each area of your life is affected by this calmness and focus.

You become focused on internal forces which you know are the key to powerful striking forces in combat.

Mind body connection.

Smooth moves—lightening speed.

Glide.

If you never give up—you are unbeatable.

Control is yours when you want it.

Water softly flows down hill however, it can cut through solid rock, you flow like water.

Know your limits.

Strength is yours, pure confidence.

High self belief is set at default.

Hitting, kicking, throwing and grappling become merged in a graceful oneness of movement.

Your life has balance.

Your focus has pinpoint accuracy.

You are a wise, peaceful warrior. Wise warriors are non aggressive. Wise warriors have unrivalled fighting manoeuvres. You have combat efficiency.

Your punches channel internal energy into your opponent, causing imbalance in them.

You develop a sense of unguarded openings in your opponents' repertoire and use that weakness effectively.

You have mental clarity and calmness of mind.

Your movements are fast and direct.

Imagine

Now I want you to imagine a situation where you have incurred some sort of conflict, it might be in competition or perhaps on the street. If on the street the person is trying to start a fight with you. As a martial arts practitioner you avoid conflict when possible, this is a truth. You now consider your options to leave the situation without using physical force. The situation deteriorates and it is clear that you will need to use your combat abilities to protect yourself. Run through this scenario to a successful conclusion. You can decide on the final outcome because you are in control.

If you are imagining a situation in competition you are able to initiate the fight as it still remains a challenge on your abilities.

Your training and humble attitude allow you to remain calm and composed with a mental stability to assist you in your goal. All the suggestions you have previously heard are true. That's right and you accept these without question.

Now continue on this journey in your mind, revealing confidence and power in your abilities.

Your every act is supreme, you are calm yet fast to react, sharp focused, awesome.

Continue until you have come to a satisfactory conclusion, when you have won the confrontation. Notice your feelings of relief and pride.

Notice the sounds and smells that surround you. You realise you have the abilities you require.

Rugby Football

▼

'…Never to stop dreaming. Because my success started in a dream and dreams can come true if you apply your mind. The way to go about it is never to lose your dream. If you lose your dream then you've got nothing to work for.'
—Francois Pienaar, Captain of the Springboks, South African Rugby World Cup winners.
—'Reflections on Success' by Martyn Lewis, Lennard Publishing.

Introduction

As with all team sports the Rugby player can develop countless problems in the game, this book and in particular this script is written with some of the most usual 'problems' in mind. Re-write the scripts to make it more personal to your own style and problem areas. I will give you some common general suggestions plus a few suggestions that are focused on particular needs of specific players and their expected strengths.

Script

Pass only to people who are in better playing positions than yourself.

Good timing equals good tackling.

Kick the ball with precision, aim and power.

Dummy side steps work well, you weave…

Side stepping and weaving are an effective way to beat an opponent.

You have the foresight to put yourself in the best position possible for good play. This gives you as a team the advantage.

Gain control of your opponents side of the pitch as much as possible.

Your team move as a powerful wave of good tactical rugby.

You are ready for the unexpected.

You realise your qualities for success and use them to their fullest.

You are clear of your motivations and ambitions and these install determination in your attitude. Far more than before.

Your fans are amazed at your effective play.

Perform as a team.

Forwards and backs work independently and as a team.

Stamina is based in the mind you now programme endless stamina in to your subconscious for easy access when required.

Your inner confidence has emerged.

You are strengthened to deal with any situation.

You project confidence in the way you feel and behave. It's true, you know this.

Scrummaging, and lineout techniques work out well.

Each player plays their part perfectly.

Perform as a team.

The opposition have weaknesses, although underestimating them would be wrong.

Your instinct for your opponents weaknesses and favourite moves makes you a powerful opponent.

When catching keep your eye on the ball until you have it in your possession.

The forwards

Hooker.

Your supporting role enables you to gain possession of the ball in the scrum.

Your abilities to support the props are immense, you are a tower of strength, you know this.

Passing and receiving the ball is easy for you.

Prop.

You are the strongest player on the field, this is your role in the game.

You support the scrum with your strong rugged ability.

You are a powerhouse.

Hold the scrum together, you are the foundation.

The opposition are weak, but under estimating them would be wrong.

Flanker.

Think quickly in the scrum, make a break rapidly.

Produce an increase in your work-rate during the scrum.

Intelligent play is important to you.

You have good tackling skills.

Lock.

In the lineout you gain possession, it's easy for you to gain control of the ball.

You have endless jumping abilities, your thighs are like coiled springs ready to unleash their power.

You have dexterity with quality ball handling skills.

No.8.

You are the key team player, you work well as a team.

Your thighs are like coiled springs ready to unleash their power upon request.

You manage scrums and line outs with clarity and foresight.

Direct with confidence.

You have a sixth sense for the way a game is directing.

The Backs

Scrum half.

You are the best all rounder in the game.

Strong accurate passes are yours.

Pick the ball off the ground quickly and surely, pass it briskly with direction.

Your training has developed a faultless performance in your game.

Get the ball away from the scrum quickly.
Motivate your side.

Determination.

You have good handling skills.

Pick up the ball quickly and pass to one of your players.

Kick well and accurately.

Tackle with courage and determination.

Fly half.

Control the game.

You have a sixth sense for play, you have focus.

Think quickly when in possession of the ball.

Gain your team advantage.

Tackle the opposition with confidence.

Hit hard and confidently in your tackles.

Centre.

A competent all rounder, tackling, running, handling the ball and kicking are attributes you possess.

Make quick decisions with the ball.

Take and give accurate passes.

Remain composed when faced with attacking forwards.

Winger.

The man with the sprinting abilities, you move with leopard like reflexes.

Keep your eyes on the ball, catch with clarity and gain the ball when possibly.

Advance upfield swiftly with confidence.

Keep scoring tries, this is your job.

Run, weave, side-step and avoid being tackled by defenders.

Pass the ball when team mates are in a better position than you.

Full-back.

Attack and defend.

Keep your eye on the ball, your job is reacting, anticipating and catching the ball.

You have dexterity, catching bouncing balls is easy.

Defence–it's up to you.

Take kicks easily.

Tackle with confidence, go in hard.

Imagine

You now imagine yourself just before a match, in the changing rooms, you are mentally prepared, your mind is focused on the game.

Your team mates are motivated and supportive. You feel confident in your own abilities and those of your team. You now begin to get ready for the game, put on your clothing, boots and the things you'd usually do to get prepared for a game.

(leave a few minutes here to visualise the scenes)

It's now time to leave the changing rooms and walk to the pitch, you can hear the crowds cheering for you as you approach. What a wonderful feeling of pride.

Notice your feelings, notice the sounds and smells as you run onto the pitch. The feeling of your posture as you stride with confidence, pride and a determination towards a win.
You are focused on the game ahead.

Silky Soccer Skills

'Football is a game played with the arms, legs, and shoulders—but mostly from the neck up.'
—Knute Rockne 1888-1931

Introduction

It is important in team sports to make sure that everyone is aware of their role in the game before each match. The changing rooms or on the coach prior to the match are ideal places to go through some of the points and to use visualisation. This is the time when everyone in the team is together and the coach and physios etc can instil some team spirit all at the same meeting. Team spirit is very much a part of the game, and can be responsible in wining or losing the match. Emotions are responsible for more than just arousal levels, but also the release of hormones such as testosterone.

One related area of team morale is the teams strip and name. Clearly most football teams regard advertising revenue as a key aspect of the kits design and little consideration is given further than that. Colours and images on a team strip can provoke many different emotional states in them and their opposition, it could end up being the key component in a good or bad season.

The name of a team is a huge boost to team spirit and important to the fan base. Names should be altered to project an image of competence. Animal mechanical type images such as lightening fast leopards, or rockets have surprisingly positive results. This is true whatever the image sought whether it's to portray a calm, accurate image or a fast powerful tactical one.

The aspect of names can also come down to a personal level for individual players. Football players are notorious for giving each other 'amusing', mickey taking names which boost moral on and off the pitch. By selectively changing some of these names, the coach can give an increased sense of worth and skill to particular players. Fighting images can create a boost during match play. When the player is referred to by a positive name, an increase in adrenaline can sometimes be seen when the self-image and the projected self-image collide.

Years of research by James Bruning of Ohio University has discovered many prejudices and assumptions in the social world about peoples names, even before the studied person was met. Some names were perceived as being more masculine or feminine on both male and female sides. James found that people were even considered (or not) for a job interview on the mere impact upon a candidates name on their Curriculum Vitae.

The celebrity ranks are awash with examples of people who had been less than successful in projecting a worthy image or trying to become famous previous to changing their name. Priscilla White became Cilla Black, Cliff Richard was formerly Harry Webb there are countless examples from all walks of life including the sporting arena that illustrate the powerful benefits in names and self image.

Script

You walk out on to the pitch with a great sense of pride and a great sense of pleasure in the Strip that you are wearing, what a wonderful feeling.

You will find yourself moving with calmness and confidence, your body language projects an air of quiet confidence to the opposition which unnerves them.

There will be many opportunities for you to attain the ball today, you select the ones that you feel can be most beneficial.

You work as a team supremely well.

The accuracy of your play will amaze both your fans and your opponents.

Any past weaknesses in your style are corrected and developed to your advantage.

You will find yourself moving with a calm confidence at lightening speed, with cat like reflexes when required.

Your supporters will be amazed at your brilliance, at your ability to anticipate your opponents every move.

Close ball skills and quick foot work works well for you.

Your inner confidence has emerged.

You are strengthened to deal with any situation.

Perform as a team.

There are no ends to your limits. You are more agile, quicker and better than your opponents.

Pressurise your opponent with a high work rate.

Surge forwards towards their goal.

You approach confrontation with calmness, and positively that is a winning combination, you keep your cool.

Focus on the ball, you view it with ease, you notice it's texture, colour, the noise of boot on ball and the sound it makes on the grounds surface.

Your inner confidence has emerged.

When the opportunity arises you are prepared, you are in the correct place and anticipate the balls next position with ease.

You are bigger, better, stronger, quicker and more agile than your opponents, this is clear to you. Your training has paid off, you have the qualities of success.

The ball is passed with accurate self-assurance.

Your legs are strong and powerful, with an almost machine like accuracy and control on the ball. When you kick the ball it reaches its target quickly and efficiently.

Seeing, anticipating, reacting is your job.

You project confidence in the way you play.

You are steady and quick footed at all times.

Determination and motivation is yours.

You are a team of talented winners.

Winning is your main objective.

You have lightening reactions and anticipate your opponents moves with ease.

There are no ends to your limits. You are quicker, bigger and better than your opponents.

Make it happen, you are in control.

By knowing where to move, your game becomes far easier to win and you achieve the results that your team aspire too. You are a team of committed winners, this is your time.

Each player plays their part elegantly.

Goal Keeper.

Protects his ground with the knowledge that nothing can pass him. He predicts the balls line of movement and intercepts with speed. He can reach all corners of his box effortlessly and in plenty of time.

Last line of defence—it's up to you. Something your team mates find difficult you can do.

You are a fearless keeper. Make friends with the ball, it works for you. The ball is on your side, it's there for you.

Your abilities to determine ball travel are switched on to maximum.

With your flexibility you can reach any area of the box. You have the elasticity.

Stay relaxed, a relaxed level of body and mind enables you to make competent discussions.

All attempts at the goal are easy to defend. You can intercept any manoeuvre.

Defenders.

Protect the keeper, work as a team.

You predict how much room the opponents strikers are allowed—this is your domain. Take charge.

Take notice of your coaches advice and in particular the advice of your captain—he has the foresight.

Work the chosen formation, which ever formation your team are playing—make it watertight.

This works well for you.

Flat line defence creates an unpassable wall.

A sweeper formation boxes your keeper in from attack, your team mates link with chain like security.

You dominate over attacking players, approach them with confidence.

Mid fielders Wingers.

Remember your coach's advice, act on that advice.

You depict the tempo of the game, you are in control, you have the confidence to make these decisions.

You are the teams natural speed regulator, choosing and anticipating the pace with unforeseen clarity.

Anticipating and reacting are your goals.

Set up play for your team mates.

Read the game, you have this sixth sense.

Be in the right place at the right time on the field.

Gain possession of the ball.

You are a slick all rounder.

Your strategies work well, you release wingers and strikers with a well weighted ball, lob or a driving run into the box—it's your choice.

Gain possession quickly. Keep your eye on the ball at all times.

Read the game so you are in the correct position at all times.
You have a sixth sense for intelligent play.
Anticipation and dictation are yours, you are setting up play for your team supremely well.
Your intelligent play drags away your opponents defending leaving space for the strikers to score. The team work in unison.
You all have your individual roles and abilities that fuse together in a dynamic oneness.
Your team have the confidence to work well of you.
When required you back track to assist your defence with play. You react and anticipate play with ease.
Reserves of energy are yours to draw upon. It's there when you need it.
Set up good quality play.

Centre forwards / strikers.

Set up your teams play, lightening reflexes, accurate confident passes.
You score goals.
Gain possession quickly—work as a team.
Last position on pitch.
You have flexible play.

Fast movers.

Always on the move, rocket speed.
Run onto the ball with lightening reflexes.
Smash those defences, you can do this.
Speed is yours—right place at the right time, you have this ability.
Something that used to be difficult is very easy for you.
You have a sixth sense for intelligent play.
Control the ball—score.

Positional strikers.

Always in the right place at the right time.

Anticipating the balls direction is easy for you.
Gain possession with ease.
Panther like speed.

Captain.

You are in control, this is your game.

Lead with authority and confidence. You always make the right decisions at the right time.

On and off the pitch you are the captain. You work well as a team.

You boost morale and motivate your team, you work well with your coach.

On the pitch you take charge.

You set a silky like example of quality play.

Keep a regimented formation through good communication with your players.

Elevate the games play consistently. There is always room at the top.

Now I want you to set a conditioned response mechanism in your mind, a response that will have the effect of producing the internal settings required for you to play to your best ability. When the whistle blows you will replicate the bodily conditions that you have had in the past when you played supremely well. If you have trouble finding a situation that you excelled in, imagine a splendid moment when one of your sporting heroes played to the best of their ability, and imagine being that player, step inside their body.

When you hear that starting whistle the sound acts as a trigger to your body and mind, a trigger that tells you unconsciously to achieve the arousal levels that you require to excel at football. And you do.

You have the energy reserves to assist you in your goals.
Control the ball.
Score.

Work individually and as a tem supremely well.

Imagine

Imagine sitting in the changing rooms before a big game, your coach is there, your team-mates and everyone else who should be there.

The whistle blows and you feel wonderful. You have the motivation and energy to achieve your goals, and you do.
Your sporting arousal levels are set to supreme.

Sports Fear Control

'You're afraid of losing, you're afraid of not being successful, but at the same time your opposition are just as frightened of you as you are of them. You've got to make them believe that they're more afraid of you than you are of them.'
—Linford Christie, Olympic 100 metre sprint Gold medallist.
'Reflections on Success' by Martyn Lewis, Lennard Publishing.

Introduction

Many people get a little confused as to which emotions they are experiencing and often label their emotions incorrectly. Anxiety, fear, nervousness, excitement and tension are areas which are easily confused. It's a shame to think that someone could be feeling nervous excitement about an event when they are labelling the emotion fear. This does occur, the solution is easy, acknowledge and relabel the emotion. When you next feel fear, tell yourself in your own mind or out loud, "I will remain calm and composed, I will enjoy these feelings of excited anticipation towards my approaching competition". When you learn to catch the emotions and relabel them as you wish, you start to enjoy the experiences and notice that you have fewer unpleasant ones. All human experience is a matter of perception, you can learn to perceive events in whichever way you choose.

Sadam Hussain and Mother Teresa have the same neurology, but their perceptions and therefore experiences are light years apart. Consequently their behaviour is somewhat different. This is often seen in the danger seeking extreme sports person too. Many people would be full of fear and trepidation from the mere thought of jumping off a 500-foot waterfall. The extreme sports person relishes the adrenaline rush and feelings of accomplishment in pushing their mind and bodies to their limits. Physically these are the same human beings as the fearful athlete, their bodies have no real differences, but their internal dialogue and the way they view events are totally different. You can learn this too.

Script

You have overwhelming confidence in your own abilities.

Your life develops into series of successes.

You begin to become aware of your need to enjoy experiencing unfamiliar situations, so that you can continue the development of your ever maturing personality.

Each time that you meet a new situation, you approach it with calm, relaxed, confident curiosity. You relish in the possibility of personal development that these situations bring.

You have a huge level of respect and appreciation for yourself and your abilities.

The best way to fight fear is to confront it, action in spite of fear is the way forwards.

You breathe calmly and deeply, which has the physiological effect of relaxing your system.

Your face reflects an inner tranquillity, a calm level of confidence, because you are confident.

Your body and mind are focused on the job at hand.

With your new level of relaxation you have the ability to remain calm and focused in competitive situations. You adjust your arousal levels to be the most effective in attaining your goals.

With everyday that passes, you get closer and closer to an important event so your confidence grows.

You get better and better.

You have many positive attributes, focus upon these.

Activate your natural stress release mechanisms in your mind and body.

You are a self-confident winner.

You replace your old recordings of nervousness and replace them with optimism and enthusiasm in pursuing your goals. Focus upon your goals.

As your thinking becomes more positive, you go about your life in a naturally calm manner.

Now I'm going to give you a key word to use as a trigger, and when you say this word to yourself, it will have the effect of relaxing you. It will have an effect of releasing all the tension and anxiety that you may have. You will say this word whenever you feel the need, whenever you are feeling a little nervous or anxious.

Your conditioned response word is "winner" you say the word "winner" and this makes you calm, relaxed and focused on your goal, your body becomes relaxed but your mind stays sharp and alert.

'Winner' you are a 'winner'.

Imagine

Imagine yourself as you prepare to compete, you are dressed to compete, those people who should be around are there supporting you.

You slowly take three deep breaths and begin to relax. You are much more relaxed than at previous events. The sessions of hypnosis that you have been using have had a wonderful effect of eliminating past negative fears.

You are going to be successful, you are sure of this.

You feel confident and relaxed because you have prepared so well.

You relax up until your competition and access the correct level of arousal when the event begins, it's easy for you.

Your trigger word is "winner".

Carry on visualising the event that you are about to enter, watch yourself compete at your best ever.
Watch and hear, totally experience the sensations involved in winning, the noise of the cheering crowd, the feelings of pride and accomplishment. Enjoy it. Run this movie all the way through in your mind until you have finished.

(Do it now—leave gap)

Now do this again but this time instead of watching yourself from a distance, run through your successful competition from the point of actually being there, see it through your own eyes, step into the image of your body that you watched previously.

Sports Success Programming

'I found out that fear itself is what causes a person to think about all the bad things that can happen. …I know that fear is the only thing that prohibits you from being the very best you can be.'
—Evander Holyfield, three times Heavy Weight Champion of the World. 'What is enlightenment? Magazine', issue 15, interview by Andrew Cohen.

Introduction

This script is a more general script for sports success, you are urged to add and take away elements that are appropriate or not to your sports activities. Some of these can also be added to other scripts in this book. If a quote just somehow jumps out at you, use it in your script. Often this is a way in which your subconscious mind communicates that this area needs improving even though it is out of your intellectual awareness, it might be the reason for unconscious success sabotage.

The traits you need mentally, emotionally and physically you already possess within. With the assistance of hypnosis you are able to gain access to these abilities.

By using hypnotic visualisation you are already experiencing the reality of your success, the mind is real, thoughts are real. You are capable of being the person you wish to be.

Script

You now begin programming the computer of your mind.

You have developed a deep feeling of certainty, a great sense of confidence.

You reject all thoughts that are detrimental to your development and attainment of success.

You are a magnet for success.

You attract the people and circumstances that will assist you in achieving your goals.

You develop the courage to face the opportunities and fears that you have had in the past this will enable you to grow and move closer to your goals.

Your thoughts and feelings are success power reactors of the mind.

Only positive thoughts enter your mind.

You are a natural points accumulator.

Your training has paid off, this gives you confidence.

It is your natural right to be successful.

Your brain waves are tuned to natural success.

You are becoming richer everyday.

You are a success magnet.

Your ideas and activities grow with eachday that passes. It's easy for you.

You feel more calm, more confident in your abilities to be a success. Success is increasing in your life and everyday your goals become closer and closer.

You feel the excitement of reaching your goals and aspirations. Nothing is too good for you, you can have it all.

You are bigger, and better than your opponents.

You are strong enough to deal with any situation that occurs.

Your instinct for your opponents weaknesses makes you a powerful force.

Endurance and strength are based in the mind, you have this power of mind, it's yours when you need it.

Confidence is projected in your posture and sports style.

You release your qualities for success.

You project confidence in the way you feel and behave.

You are ready for the unexpected and deal with it calmly.

You accept your natural right to be successful.

Your supporters are amazed at your brilliance.

There are no ends to your abilities.

Sport is a part of your own personal development.

You are supreme at anticipating and reacting to difficult situations. You are a winner who achieves their goals.

You feel excitement about reaching your goals and aspirations.

You become better with each day that passes.

Only positive thoughts enter your mind.

Imagine

Imagine yourself being the person you wish to be, doing the things you want to excel at. Imagine the thoughts, feelings and sounds you would have.

STYLE IMPROVEMENT

'Losers have tons of variety. Champions take pride in just learning to hit the same old boring winners!'

—Vic Braden.

Introduction

In most cases style improvement is relatively straightforward, any fault in style is often down to sloppiness. It is all to easy too fall into bad physical habits when becoming proficient at a chosen sport. These style problems, like all behaviours, are based in the mind, so hypnosis is the obvious solution. By using in-trance visualisation techniques we can change the body's performance and correct physical problems.

Input from your sports coach is often a great help here because he can see aspects that are out of your vision. Athletic style is an aspect which is difficult to analyse by oneself, so if you don't have a coach get some advice from a friend.

When visualising your improved style performances, do so as if you are a perfect performer, you might like to pretend actually being in the body of an athlete that you admire. Role-play in your mind exactly what you'd see, feel, hear and act like, above all enjoy the whole experience.

Scripts

Examine in your mind and correct any faults in your sports performance.

You play in the manner you wish to play, perfect form is yours.

Your body moves with confidence.

Your new confident posture has a positive effect on your game.

You release your true potential which has been laying dormant in your mind.

You are a winner, a natural points accumulator.

You have self-discipline in your training, this helps eliminate past sloppiness in your style.

You are a talented athlete with the skills you need within you.

You benefit greatly from your self-image.

You become disassociated from negative influences.

You have independence and positive perceptions of personal control. You are in control.

Your thoughts and feelings are success power reactors of the mind.

Only positive thoughts enter your mind.

You relax more in your life, something that used to be difficult is now very easy.

With each day that passes, athletic style improvements increase.

Imagine

Imagine yourself playing the way you wish to play, achieving perfect performance, perfect style. Feel the way you would feel and react.

Notice the people around you, their reactions to your perfect style and elite performance…

Run through your performance from a disassociated view, from a distance. Once reviewed 'go inside' your own body (or that of someone you admire) and review the same scenario through the eyes of the athlete.

Supreme Weight Loss

'I've always got to look good, because one of the most important parts of being an athlete is to look the part. If you look like an athlete you scare the hell out of everybody else and that's half your work.'
—Linford Christie, Olympic 100 metre sprint Gold medallist.
'Reflections on Success' by Martyn Lewis, Lennard Publishing.

Introduction

All symptoms have an unconscious benefit, weight control is no exception. Before suggestion therapy is started it is good practice to establish the individual benefits that clients receive from being overweight. Once this is defined it is easy to collapse the process instantly and receive long lasting results. Aspects in the following scripts have been used to gain dramatic results in cosmetic weight loss, often without diet or exercises alterations. This form of hypnosis always confirms to me the unlimited power of our psyches. Mind control aside, the main physiological benefit in weight control is to acknowledge that a calorie is merely a unit of energy. This realisation enables you to review food from being a form of pleasure or means of emotion elevation to a fuel for your body. This way it will seem ridiculous to intake large amounts of energy fuel if you are not utilising the energy through exercise. This is a very profound distinction.

For more on weight loss please see previous chapters.

Scripts

You can now see why you have been unable to change and attain your goals of having a slim and shapely body, from this new relaxed perspective, it is so clear.

Imagine your body as it is, and the decision that you are going to lose that excess body fat through diet and exercise.

You are going to change your eating patterns to such an extent that it becomes easy for you, weight loss is inevitable.

Weight loss actually becomes enjoyable for you, its fun, you are a successful achiever. You enjoy losing weight because you eat meals more slowly, thus you begin to enjoy food even more, certainly much more than before. The slower you eat your food, and the more selective in the types of food you consume, the more you can enjoy the food you eat.

Energy in—energy out.

You will only eat at meal times, and the more strict you become on this rule of only eating at meal times, the more pride and pleasure you gain from losing that excess weight.

It surprises you at how much pride you feel in the smaller portions you select for yourself at meal times. It pleases you to be able to leave excess. You do find it easy to push food away when your body decides you have had enough.

Food is fuel for the body and mind, this is the new view you have, it is good quality fuel.

You're only going to eat at meal times, and at meal times you will find yourself taking a lot of pride and pleasure in maintaining your correct body weight through sensible eating.

You have control. Self control is yours when you want it.

You consume fewer calories than you burn until you reach your ideal weight, and once you reach it you will maintain it.
You select the quality of food rather than quantity, so that you can enjoy your food more, much more than before. And it's fun!
Remember when you take something away it makes it more desirable, so the less food you consume the more you will appreciate and enjoy the smaller amounts that you eat.

The less you eat the more you enjoy your food. So you do eat enough food for your daily requirements.

You can drop sugar and white bread completely from your diet if you wish to, but only if you feel that would help.

As you go deeper and deeper into relaxation, with every breath that you take, all the sounds fade away in the distance. You will pay attention only to the sounds of my voice, listening carefully to the suggestions that I give you.

This programme is designed so that you will permanently lose all your excess fat, and become a lean, alert and vigorous person. You will lose all your excess weight and keep it off, easily and comfortably.
You will become a new person, in a new lean form, with new eating habits, and a new positive self-image.

Negative experiences act only as a foundation to your future success.

I don't know how long it will be before you notice your new eating habits, and how contented you become, but you do.

You are going to enjoy life eating only when you have physiological needs for food, both now, and for the rest of your life.

You are becoming healthier and healthier, better and better with each day that passes.

In the past you were eating more than your body needed for its energy requirements, you stored this extra energy as inert fat. In order to lose weight and reduce this inert fat, you burn it up as you meet your daily requirements for energy.

You eat less than you require each day and lose weight.

Later when you are lean, you will eat only that amount that you need for your physiological needs each day. But for right now, you are developing habits to consume fewer calories than you are using, that amount will vary from day to day and depend greatly on your daily activities.

You will eat less than you need because the storage of excess fat will make up for the difference. This will cause the fat stores to be burnt and you will lose weight.

You are going to eat a great deal less than in the past, but it will be enough to satisfy you.

You will eat less and burn the extra fat. You will turn this inert fat into energy. From now on you are going to form a new eating pattern, a pattern that will almost be a compulsion, until you reach your ideal weight.

Fat by its very nature contains an extremely large amount of stored energy. So, if you burn a little every day, you will lose only a little weight everyday. Weight loss needs to be gradual, but it needs to be consistent. A loss of two to four pounds per week is ideal. When your excess weight is off, it's off for good.

You are a new person, about to emerge from a cocoon padded with fat. Be happy with your new form. Emerge as a new person with thoroughly changed ideas, a thoroughly changed self-image, and altered patterns of behaviour.

Relax and let all of these suggestions sink into your mind as an image, this image is of good quality, tasty food. Food you enjoy. There will always be plenty of it. For you, there will always be enough food. There is plenty of food everywhere. With all this food readily available, the need to store any excess food inside and around your body is eliminated. There is plenty of food.

There is plenty of the right kinds of food, all the kinds that your body needs when it needs it. From now on you will eat only the very things your body needs. You are through with storing pads and rolls of excess fat.

A loss of two to four pounds of fat per week is ideal, until you come down to your ideal weight.

Excess fat makes you unattractive, so you change this. Fat ruins and shortens your life, so you start to lose weight from this day on until you reach your ideal weight.

There is plenty of food all around you, you have reduced the need to store food in the form of excess body fat.

There is in your central brain a small area which regulates the biochemistry of your body and it controls the amount of fat you store in your body. You can control this area through the subconscious mind, it controls your weight by controlling your body's biochemistry. Hypnosis can influence your subconscious mind to alter the control of both your appetite and the storage of food in the form of fat.

Now whilst you are under the influence of hypnosis, I'm going to give you some suggestions that will change your body's biochemistry enabling you to break up your stores of excess fat. These suggestions will break up and eliminate forever your excess stores of fat.

Burn fat as energy, get rid of your excess fat in every healthy way possible. It metabolises quite readily. You can imagine the fat melting away as you use it as energy. The globules of fat storage are leaving the normal cells and being carried away. The fat is being burnt up, do you realise this process has already begun?

You will now use your stored fat to supply energy. This is extra energy to make you more vigorous. As you are eliminating the excess fat, you will eat far less than you need each day, for the extra calories are coming from the food you ate yesterday and last week. You and only you is in control of your eating habits, so if you are offered food by someone else, you refuse it if your body has already consumed its required amount to assist you in losing weight.

You want this ugly fat to be gone forever, so you resist other people offering you excess food. These excess stores of fat are gone forever. They were bad for your health and well being. You need to get rid of them, just as an over loaded ship needs to get rid of excess cargo.

You will only eat small amounts until you have used all of this stored energy and all of those ugly stores of excess fat are gone. From this moment on you are going to eat less, consequently becoming more and more active, for you feel better than you have felt before.

You are going to reach your ideal weight for your height and you'll do it healthily.

You eat smaller quantities and better quality food until your weight has come down to the lean size that you require. Then you will eat sensibly and correctly for the rest of your life.
You will eat sensibly, get plenty of exercise and drink adequate liquids to make you feel healthy, lean, trim and desirable.

After you changed your biochemistry you have changed your whole body and your feelings to that of a wonderful sense of well being. You eat sensibly, get plenty of exercise, drink adequate liquids to make you feel healthy, lean, trim and desirable.

You are going to find something that used to be difficult is now ridiculously simple. It's certainly easy for you.

Food and energy burning is controlled by specific areas in your brain, these areas regulate your metabolism, areas that you and only you can direct to work in the way you wish.

Already we have been able to visualise the way in which you want to look physically. Mental pictures have been created in your mind of the body that you wish to attain. And you are aware that it has become easy to achieve with the help of your subconscious mind, with the help of hypnosis. You don't have to know the way in which your body and mind works, just picture that excess weight melting away.

You have now directed your mind to lose the weight you wish to lose. It's true.

Now imagine yourself in front of a full length mirror, imagine your body the way you wish it to be, with the confident posture that you will achieve with such a perfect body, at the weight you desire.

The thought of the excess fat that you once had and the poor quality high quantity food you once consumed disgusts you.

You know that all of the changes in your life that you require have begun. You do look a lot slimmer already, remember we are seeking leanness not thinness, and you are becoming very lean indeed.

You become very proud at the comments that you receive from family and friends from their admiration that you have accomplished your goals. You can imagine how pleased they are for you, how fitter, healthier and more energetic they see you as being. And you are all of these things.

What a wonderful body you have, and every time you realise you are reaching your target weight and with each day that passes you feel a tremendous feeling of achievement, satisfaction and complete confidence in your abilities.

Many foods that you have desired in the past are bad for you, and quite fattening. Some of the foods are good for you. You begin to become more and more aware of which is which, which foods will help you feel energetic and healthy and which will only fuel excess fat. You start to cut out fattening foods from your diet.

The foods that are good for you taste so much better because attached to these foods are feelings of pride and accomplishment and an increased sense of health and well being.

Athlete's predominately eat good quality healthy food.

We agreed earlier that our bodies and minds have special ways of metabolising foods, and we decided that we were capable of directing these metabolic behaviours. Now, I want you to imagine a 'switch' responsible for food metabolism in your mind. Turn this switch to the 'on' position. Turn the switch 'on' in your mind and leave it 'on'. This creates a super power of burning energy that makes it very difficult for your body to store excess surplus fat.

Super power in your mind.

Remember energy in, energy out, you need to exercise.

The molecules and particles of your body are burning all the excess fat that you once consumed and weight loss becomes amazingly and unbelievable simple for you. This is because your unconscious mind is assisting you all the way.

You become the weight you wish to be.

Healthier and healthier.

You lose weight.

This switch that you have just turned to the 'on' position in your mind, has an effect of making all the stored excess fat around your body to become mobile. Fat cells flow freely and are burnt quickly as fuel increasing your vitality. The excess energy that you once stored becomes mobile and flows out of your body. You lose weight.

When this session is over you are going to feel as good as you are feeling now, especially about your new eating habits. You will wake up to full consciousness when this session is over but will remain feeling as good as you do now about your weight loss, inspired, motivated.

When you consider your new eating habits you will experience an overwhelming feeling of satisfaction and excitement in your new improved, streamlined goals.

Eating less and exercising more now becomes a fun goal of yours, almost a compulsion.

You find yourself eating the portions that a normal sized person would to retain a healthy body size.

You only eat as much as you need to, food is a source of fuel for your body and mind. You stop regarding it as a means to elevate your emotions or eliminate boredom. Food is your body's fuel, you eat only to fuel your body.

Hypertrophy is easy for you.

I don't know how long it will take for you to realise that you have already begun to lose weight, or that your habits have changed so dramatically and instantly, but that's OK, as long as you achieve your goal of losing that excess weight.

Your subconscious mind assists you in your goals.

You are allowed to be amazed at the results you attain in the next couple of months, it is a superb achievement, no matter how easy it is.

You now make friends with your body, because in the past you have not been totally honest with yourself, and something that used to be difficult is now amazingly simple.

You decide that you will listen to the part of your brain that tells you that you are full, and stops you from eating more than your body requires.

You realise that your appetite has previously been driven by your emotions rather than your hunger. It is correct to eat when your appetite says, 'I'm hungry'. But you have been eating out of habit, you have been eating to satisfy psychological and emotional cravings. You must start paying attention to your appetite when it tells you 'I'm satisfied, Stop eating'.

Your appetite needs reinforcing.

Negative experiences act only as a foundation to your future success.

Tune in to your body's sensations. If you eat too much against the advice of your body, you'll violate your natural behaviours.
It's important that you eat all your physiological needs to replace your energy stores for immediate use and to store sugar. You must immediately ban any and all plans you have for crash dieting. You will do so, other wise you bring into play an old instinct for self-preservation.

It is important that you develop now the habit to eat all that you need to eat to stay healthy, you will always eat all that you need to eat. Under hypnosis, you can reinforce the normal feedback mechanisms that check and balance. The ones which communicates to you when you need food and when your appetite is satisfied.

Surprisingly, in the past your great concern about being overweight lead to sporadic dieting. This suggests starvation, starvation demands defence which brings out the instinct of self-survival. This instinct is responsible for maintaining your excess weight.

You gain the perfect body; your ideal body.

Slim people eat all they want.

Slim people do well, Slim, attractive people say, 'I eat all I want and remain slim'.

You are going to restore, through hypnosis, your normal instincts that will keep you satisfied and bring into play that wonderful feeling of well being. You can remove that thought of dieting from your day to day behaviours.
Hypnosis is a positive word, it makes you relaxed and comfortable. Hypnosis succeeds.

Diets bring about starvation which leads to overeating and obesity. Hypnosis brings about satisfaction which leads to a lean, healthy, attractive body and a relaxed peaceful mind.

You concentrate on restoring natural responses, obeying every suggestion I give you. Hypnotic suggestions which you receive rapidly bring about changes which are necessary to insure a permanently lean, healthy, attractive body.

Each time you are tempted to eat something that you know will make you fat, you will say to yourself 'no' and leave the food alone.
The rewards of being slender, more desirable, sexier, are more important to you than eating foods that you are wrong for you.

Gain a hold on your natural priorities.

Because you eat more slowly, you can enjoy your food more.

You are losing weight steadily everyday from now on. You are lean and shapely. The excess weight is melting off, just melting away and disappearing.
Your feelings are strengthened with each day that you are in control of your eating habits. You picture yourself the way you will be—lean, shapely and sexy.

Now relax and let all of the suggestions take complete and thorough effect upon your body and mind, as your body corrects your metabolism to change your body's biochemistry in every healthy way possible.
Let your 'appetite control centre' safely reduce your appetite so that excess storage of fat will be utilised as energy and burnt off. Eliminate all the excess harmful fat.

Imagine

Now I want you to imagine something for me. Imagine you can see an image of a person in the distance, and as you drift closer to that person, you notice that the person is a future image of yourself. It's you in the future after you have attained your goals and achieved your dreams of having a fat free and shapely body.

What a wonderful lean body.

You are so pleased with your new body you allow yourself to drift even closer to your future goal and into your future body that you will attain.

As you step inside this new body with a slim and shapely figure, you can feel what it's like to be your ideal weight and size. What a wonderful feeling, your body moves easily and swiftly.

As you follow these suggestions and observe the results, you will continue to look forwards eagerly and confidently to all the satisfactions which will be yours when your ideal weight is attained.

You will now lose between two and four pounds per week of excess fat, until you reach your ideal weight.

And as we come to the end of today's session, I'm going to count backwards from ten to one, and on the count of one you will awaken feeling bright, confident and inspired to attain your goals. You are pleased with your new changes.

1. Relaxed, coming on up to consciousness.
2. Listening to what I say, that's right.
3. Soon you will open your eyes.
4. Still calm and relaxed, but more alert.
5. Coming on up now.
6. Noticing the external world.
7. Almost there.
8. Feeling good, noticing the world around you.
9. Begin to open your eyes.
10. WIDE AWAKE, AND SMILE, WASNT THAT FUN?

Top Level Tennis

▼

'If you were to see a whole line of players from rankings 1 to 100 practising hitting the ball, a lot of them would hit the ball very, very well and you wouldn't really notice much difference between them. At the end of the day success boils down to the belief and confidence the individual has, and his or her ability to play the big points.'

—Tim Henman, 'Reflections on Success'
by Martyn Lewis, Lennard Publishing.

Introduction

As with any sport the psychological factor plays a vital part in a person's performance. One aspect often associated with mind control in sports is 'choking under pressure'. Psychological factors develop a tense body which has a negative effect on ones game.

I have put together a varied script for the tennis player, it focuses on a selection of problem areas that are common to the game. It is up to you to develop these scripts and add your own suggestions to tailor them to meet specific areas that you feel require attention.

Scripts

In the game of tennis the most important aspect is anticipating the ball.

Your focus and vision of the ball becomes superb, you can see the colour and texture of the ball at all times, it's clear to you.

Play each point as it comes, you are focused on winning each point as it comes. You are a points accumulator.

You play each point to win.

You are a winner.

You are a human points accumulator.

You see the ball with clarity, you anticipate the balls direction with ease and await its arrival at its destination.

Your cat like reflexes put you in a position for successful play, trust your instincts.

You anticipate your opponents every manoeuvre. It easy for you.

Anticipating and reacting to the game of tennis is your job.

You project a body language of confidence, head held high, chin up and racquet held up with your arms swinging.

You have a bounce in your step that springs you to your desired destination on the court. Your thighs are like coiled springs ready to release that condensed power when needed.

Pressurise your opponent, it's easy.

Every time your opponent deliverers a fast or difficult shot, it seems even easier to return it perfectly and this continues.

You realise how disheartened your opponent must be feeling and how your success is negatively affecting his game. He becomes focused on your exceptional performance and confident manner, this can only encourage you.

Your training and hard work has paid off.

Your mind reacts instantly to produce different strokes when you need them.

Any past weaknesses in your style are corrected and developed to your advantage.

You will find yourself moving with a calm confidence at lightening speed, with cat like reflexes.

You are focused on each match point as it comes.

Your supporters will be amazed at your excellence, at your ability to anticipate your opponents every move.

The more a particular shot used to upset you, the more it will inspire competence in you and this can only increase.

Your inner confidence has emerged.

You have speed, co-ordination and a winning style.

You are strengthened to deal with any situation.

You have developed the perfect stroke.

You return the ball perfectly each time without exception.

You anticipate every shot, you have complete visibility of the ball.

Your lightening like reflexes deliver you to the ball's final position before it arrives.

Imagine

Imagine now that you see yourself in a game, you crouch ready to start play. You have complete confidence that you are going to anticipate your opponents play even before he hits the ball.

Imagine yourself relaxed but focused on your game. Visualise the colours of the court, the net and rackets. Consider the noise that the ball makes as it whizzes through the air, the noise as it ricochets on the court cracking against your racket. You return the perfect shot with ease. You can feel the force of the ball on the racket, the tension through your arm, back and leg muscles as your whole body assists you in your game. It feels good to have your body and mind working in harmony.

When you are playing in a tournament and there are bystanders watching your game, imagine their admiration and applause as you play to the best of your ability.

To help you to gain the correct posture and playing style, you allow yourself to imagine watching someone you admire perhaps someone famous who plays at the level you wish to be. Imagine how that person feels, imagine how focused they become during play, and imagine the bodily sensations and emotional reactions they experience. Feel it as if that person is you. Hold their beliefs.

Weight Gain for Bodybuilding

▼

'Unless my mind triggers the will to improve my physique, it won't happen. Essentially, the mind is the master potentiator in bodybuilding.'
—Tom Platz, Mr Universe,
'Pro-style Bodybuilding', Sterling Publishing co., Inc.

Introduction

More and more people are beginning to become obsessed with their weight and muscle size. Dysmorphia is a pathological obsession with gaining muscle size. In men this is an obsession easily fallen into, in particular men often have a unrealistic perception of their chest size, they feel it is too small. There are a number of key issues in weight gain. Points very similar to those in weight loss. One key to weight gain is to remember that it is not easy, in fact in many ways it is far more difficult to put weight on than to lose it. Gaining weight is neither easy or pleasant, you must constantly consider your eating habits and prepare food in advance. The weight-gaining individual also finds himself feeling uncomfortable, sometimes almost ready to be sick, this is because of the amount of calorific intake required.

One important aspect to quick weight gain is to eat six small meals per day. Large amounts of food in the stomach is undesirable as it drains energy, therefore one needs to eat breakfast early in the morning leaving plenty of time during the day to fit other meals in. Another aspect to eating breakfast is that it kick-starts the metabolism early in the morning thus giving the athlete more weight building time. It is not possible to consume all of the nutrients in food when we over load the stomach because the body only requires a certain amount at one time, so large meals are a waste of food, waste simply gets converted to fat.

Bodybuilders almost always seem obsessed by training. Few realise that a good diet is far more important than the actual training at the gym, it is the rest and recuperation which is the key element in muscle building. In the gym you put the stress upon the muscle which breaks it down, out of the gym you want your body to enter an anabolic state to produce the muscles you desire. So if it's a case of missing one training session or missing a meal, miss the training!

It is documented that the ability of hypnosis to increase emotional responses, also serves to release testosterone in the body, aiding muscle development. The human body is unable to alter the amount of muscle fibres it has, but can increase the size and shape of the muscle and switch its percentage of slow or fast twitch fibres.

Ultimately it is the mind that controls muscle, this includes delivery of the electrical impulses that signals the muscle to work.

View your food as a way of fuelling your body with nutrition rather than eating the things you enjoy the most, just as the weight loser should do. People have a misconception of how to eat for weight gain bodybuilding, they often stuff their faces with high fat foods. This is a mistake, it will serve to slow one down and sap vitality. The best way to put weight on is to increase your intake of carbohydrates.

You only need one gram of protein per pound of body weight, unless using performance drugs where a higher level of protein can be utilised. For these reasons it is a mistake to eat huge amounts of protein, the body does not need it to build muscle, a small amount of good quality protein and plenty of carbohydrates plus water to keep the body hydrated is the key to weight gain.

Anyone who states they cannot put on weight is incorrect, if they said it is difficult for them to put on weight, then I might agree. For some it is extremely taxing to maintain a weight gain diet, but it is possible. I have to have a huge level of commitment when I set about putting on weight., I will not go to bed until I have eaten 5000 calories. That's extremely difficult for me but it's a target that I almost always reach and I gain the benefits from doing so. This way it is possible to put on at least a pound per week a combination of both muscle and fat. It does take more discipline than most people have, you will also need a calorie intake chart to monitor your progress. When people state they can't put weight on, and it might be nice to be an easy gainer, I tell them how much I eat to get similar results. Then I ask them how much they eat. Invariably they don't even know how many calories they eat per day or the amount their body requires to stay at its consistent weight. Without these pieces of information, I'm unaware of how they are going to reach their goal, it's virtually impossible.

Another issue, although important to a lesser degree, is to cut out unnecessary calorie burning, go training but then try to reduce the amount of other activities you do. Become a little lazy for a couple of weeks, an aspect many find easy to achieve. This will serve to reduce the amount of calories burnt, so you can add a little more weight. Recuperation is a most important element to weight training, so let the body build itself up in this manner.

A top tip for quick breakfast meals, either for gaining weight or any other training diet, is to eat plenty of fruit. Bananas are superb for this, high in carbohydrates, low in fat, full of water thus plenty of energy is taken from its consumption. The great thing is that fruit is so quick and easy, no preparation is needed, ideal when time is short before work, you can eat it in the car.

The last important element many bodybuilders miss is that muscle is 70% water. Drinking water or eating fruit is an excellent way to actually help build muscle. I can almost guarantee an increase quality in muscle resulting from the consumption of water and water rich foods.

(In the following script please add the name of the muscle you wish to enhance in the blank spaces provided.)

Scripts

Your body has met its energy requirements and it has sufficient material to enlarge the cells.

Food is used as a source of energy for the cells of your body especially to synthesise into larger cells.

Develop a structured diet program, Six small meals per day.

You have motivational focus so weight gain becomes easy for you.

In the gym you put stress on muscle, out of the gym you want your body to enter an anabolic state to produce the muscle you require.

Eat six times a days—optimising the nitrogen supplied to muscle.

Eat a small meal (a sandwich and glass of milk) before going to sleep thus consuming calories at night rather than fasting for eight hours.

Your body becomes an inspiration.

The muscles of the .... grow in size and strength every time you train.

You can visualise and feel the additional muscle fibres string across your .... building them faster than ever before. Feelings of excitement help release testosterone in your body.

As you feel your............. muscles grow quickly and easily, fat cells from around your waist and lower back are being burnt up by your body to use as fuel to build these huge muscles of the ....

You now realise this combination of body and mind working in harmony is very powerful and extremely effective in achieving your goals.

You become more aware of the quantity and quality of the food that you eat, and you begin to consume the correct food in the correct quantities to assist you in attaining your goals.

Consistency is the key to training and good nutrition.

Natural Growth hormones are released after heavy weight training.

Carbohydrates become your chief source of energy.

Muscles grow when you are resting and during your sleep

You build the body you dream of.

You will have the motivation to consume One Thousand calories over your daily requirements. It becomes easy to find the motivation.

You will gain over one pound per week in weight, until you reach your goal.

You build a muscular, healthy body. It's easy for you.

You begin to focus upon the quality and quantity of the food that you consume to achieve your goals.

Hypertrophy is easy for you.

You plan your daily diet in advance to assist you in gaining weight.

You mentally switch on the mechanisms that release hormones and biochemicals to assist you in gaining muscle.

Muscle building hormones are released during your sleep at night.

You recuperate from training sessions quickly and easily, your body becomes an inspiration.

Everyday and in everyway you become healthier and healthier in body and mind.

You gain a lot of pride and a lot of confidence in the speed at which you gain weight until you reach your goals.

You unleash those complex biological and hormone chemicals to assist you in your goals.

You gain atleast One pound of muscle per week, it's easy for you, you are strong and healthy.

Imagine

Imagine your body as it will become after you have attained your goals. Feel the way it moves, the heaviness, the admiration from family and friends; even strangers admire your body.

Relish the positive reactions your new physique has on others, particularly your partner, enjoy this.

Notice how confident you become in every area of your life. You are stronger, fitter, healthier than ever before and this can only increase.

NOTES

For more information about Sports Hypnosis and further advice concerning issues raised in this book visit the following websites where you can obtain links and information about qualified and experienced practitioners and related associations.

www.SuccessCoach.co.uk—Companion website of the Author—With extra scripts, Hypnosis Cd Roms, advice, reviews, books and Links.

www.SportsHypnosis.co.uk—More information about sports hypnosis, plus links to websites for mental illnesses and behavioural disorders.

Glossary of Terms

Abreaction—A term predominantly used by the Psychoanalytical school of therapy to describe the release of an unconscious anxiety producing cause thus eliminating a symptom. *(See catharsis)*

Analysand—A person partaking in analysis particularly psychoanalysis.

Auto Hypnosis—**Self Hypnosis.**

Autogenic—Self induced.

Arousal Levels—Levels of psychological and physiological alertness connected to emotions and stimuli.

Behaviour therapy—Therapy that focuses on behaviour modification rather than analysis of root causes.

***Beliefs*—Statements or opinions that we make about ourselves, others and the world. Usually involving emotional responses to these attitudes.**

Belief Systems—The underlying processes of our beliefs.

Body Language—Communication through non-verbal areas. Although not a science it can be said that the human physiology and behaviour can give clues to internal mental states, emotions and motivations. It can be misleading to take body language as 'set in stone' because it is not an exact science and can be misinterpreted.

Calorie—One unit of energy.

Catharsis—Release of anxiety resulting from the 'discovery' of a symptoms root cause.

Cognitive*—A term used to describe a vast array of mental activities these include thinking, problem solving, visualisation, beliefs and perceptions.

Cognitive Behavioural Therapy—Based upon behavioural therapy but the behaviour modification is directed slightly more towards the patients cognitive process being held responsible for their unwanted behaviour. The patients beliefs, expectations and motivations are considered to be the basis of their behaviour consequently these are modified rather than the behaviour alone. This is one of the most effective and easily monitored forms of psychotherapy.

Conscious—Generally a state of awareness of ones surroundings. In the case of the conscious mind one is referring to the part of the brain responsible for running our everyday mental life, self talk, focus of attention, perceptions and recall of memories.

Dysmorphia—Pathological obsession with gaining muscle size.

Endorphin—A naturally occurring pain relief chemical produced by the pituitary gland in the brain. This is just one endogenous opiate produced by the pituitary gland.

Hetro-hypnosis—Hypnosis administered by another i.e. by a hypnotherapist.

Hypnosis*—Altered state of consciousness, this varies due to differences in individual human states. However easily acknowledged via specific mental and physiological responses.

Hypno-analysis—Psychotherapy aided by hypnosis. Hypnosis in this case is used to gain access to unconscious causes of neurotic behaviour.

Hypnotherapy—Forms of therapy utilising hypnosis.

Hypnotic Induction—Various techniques to deliberately alter a persons state of awareness. These range from relaxation techniques to unconscious physiological inductions and pre-set triggers to access previous states.

Hypnotic Script—The suggestions used after a state of hypnosis has been administered.

Internal Dialogue—Self talk inside ones mind.

Locus of Control—A persons perception of their control over the behaviour and events in their life.

Melatonin—Pineal gland hormone often associated with sleep pattern regulation.

Modelling Behaviour—Although used in science for many years as a way to describe the process of observing and duplicating behaviour such as in social psychology. This term has more recently become synonymous with processes taught in NLP (Neuro Linguistic Programming). In NLP subjects 'copy' behaviours, beliefs and thoughts of chosen subjects who perform well in a given area, consequently the 'modeller' is said be able to duplicate the subjects results.

Motivation—Thought or feeling that 'drives' a person to act. Motivations are sometimes termed as 'Freudian style' unconscious driving forces in the form of a neurosis.

Nervous System—two main parts; Autonomic and Central.

Autonomic—regulator of some unconscious processes, split into subdivisions, *sympathetic* and *parasympathetic*.

Central—the brain, spinal cord and neural processes.

Parasympathetic System—A part of the Autonomic Nervous System, generally relaxes body parts, although there is a crossover in some instances. Among other functions it constricts pupils, slows heart rate (see also sympathetic system).

Phobia—Irrational fear of an object. Often these can develop into a fear based merely on a thought or feeling without the actual phobic object being present. The fear has a physical response of 'fight or flight' and is usually said to be based on a conditioned response to a past event.

Pituitary Gland—The gland responsible for the endocrine system. Controls many hormones, growth and the metabolism.

Pineal gland—Responsible for excretion of Melatonin and regulation of sleep. Its full functions in the human are not fully known yet.

Placebo—A substance that has no known pharmacological effect but has a strong enough effect on the patients belief system to modify behaviour or illness.

Posthypnotic Suggestion—Suggestions to a hypnotised person that he or she will behave or think in a particular manner. Usually more specifically used to describe suggestions that will trigger sometime after the state of hypnosis has been removed.

Self-hypnosis—Hypnosis administered by ones self. (*See Hetrohypnosis*)

Self-talk—(*See internal dialogue.*)

Serotonin—A neurotransmitter found in the central nervous system responsible for various functions which include sleep, pain and depression.

Somnambulistic—Although in medical terms this is defined as a 'sleep walker' in hypnosis we tend to categorise people under this term if they go into a very 'deep' level of relaxation, so much so that the just seem to sleep through a session. To the analyst and the stage performer they are one of the most difficult of participants as little reaction is observed.

Subconscious—Out of conscious awareness or immediate access.

Sympathetic system—A part of the Autonomic Nervous System that generally 'activates' body functions. Amongst other activities it dilates pupils increases heart rate and inhibits bladder contraction (see also parasympathetic system).

Symptom Substitution—Another Freudian term used to describe a situation where one 'removes' a symptom through Hypnosis or any other therapy, and the originating 'cause' still remains. Because the symptom not the cause has been removed the cause will simply create another symptom in place of the other. The theory being that the subconscious is still communicating the problem to the patient.

BIBLIOGRAPHY

Anderson, Peggy—*Great Quotes from Great Sports Heroes*. Career Press.

Bandler, Richard and Grinder, John-*Trance-formations—NLP and the structure of magic*. Real People Press.

Carr, Allen—*The only way to stop smoking permanently*—Penguin books.

Clark, Nancy—*Nancy Clark's Sports Nutrition Guidebook*—Human Kinetics Publishing.

Cunningham, Les and Ralph, Wayne—*HypnoSport*—Westwood Publishing.

Dr Persaud, Raj -*Staying Sane*—Metro books.

Erickson. H. Milton—*Mind-Body Communication in Hypnosis-The seminars, workshops and Lectures of Vol. III*—Free Association books.

Fiennes, Ranulph-*Fit For Life.*—Little Brown and Company.

French, Neil—*International Association of Hypno-Analysts—Course notes*—Psychotherapy and Hypnotherapy training.

Freud, Sigmund—*Introductory Lectures on Psychoanalysis*. Penguin books.

Kit, Wong Kiew *The complete book of Tia Chi Chuan—A comprehensive guide to the principles and practices.*—Element books Limited,1996.

Lewis, Martyn—*Reflections on Success*—Lennard Publishing.

McDermott, Ian and O'Conner, Joseph—*NLP and Health*, Published by Thorsons.

Mycoe, Stephen—**www.SuccessCoach.co.uk**

Peck, M. Scott—*The Road Less Travelled* by—Arrow books.

Robbins, Anthony—*Awaken the Giant Within*—. Fireside books, Simon & Schuster.

Stone, B. Robert—*The Secrets of Total Wellness—Mind/Body Communication*—Simon and Schuster Audio.

About the Author

Hypno-analyst, Success Coach and author Stephen has over a decade of experience in Sports and Mind Therapies.

A former University boxer and dedicated athlete his main interests lie in performance enhancement, particularly muscular development.

Steve's best selling Sports Hypnosis CD's have helped to inspire, develop and motivate athletes worldwide.

www.SuccessCoach.co.uk

Printed in the United Kingdom
by Lightning Source UK Ltd.
1791